The
Reputation
Playbook

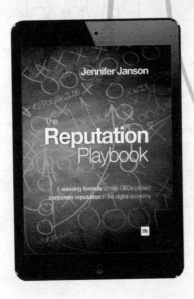

Jennifer Janson

The
Reputation
Playbook

A **winning formula** to help CEOs protect
corporate reputation in the digital economy

Hh Harriman House

HARRIMAN HOUSE LTD
18 College Street
Petersfield
Hampshire
GU31 4AD
GREAT BRITAIN
Tel: +44 (0)1730 233870
Email: enquiries@harriman-house.com
Website: www.harriman-house.com

First published in Great Britain in 2014
Copyright © Harriman House

The right of Jennifer Janson to be identified as the Author has been asserted in accordance with the Copyright, Designs and Patents Act 1988.

Paperback ISBN: 978-0-85719-355-1
Hardcover ISBN: 978-0-85719-452-7
eBook ISBN: 978-0-85719-440-4

British Library Cataloguing in Publication Data
A CIP catalogue record for this book can be obtained from the British Library.

Typeset by e-Digital Design Ltd.
Index by Indexing Specialists (UK) Ltd.
Cover and internal chalkboard images ©iStockphoto.com/traffic_analyzer
Internal layout and cover design by Harriman House/C.A.W.P.

CONTENTS

ABOUT THE AUTHOR

A Canadian who cut her communications teeth at one of the USA's biggest agencies, Jennifer Janson now owns and runs UK-based Six Degrees, a specialist reputation management agency serving the science, engineering and technology fields.

She is a strategic communicator who has worked for the likes of ABB, Ericsson, Fidelity Growth Partners Europe Lexmark, Nexans, Skype and Vodafone over her 18-year career. Jennifer is passionate about all aspects of corporate reputation and has seen time and again the damage that can be done when the true value of reputation is ignored.

Alongside running her business, Jennifer regularly gives guest lectures on reputation-related topics at University College London, Henley Business School and Buckinghamshire New University, as well as at numerous events. She is a member of the UK's Business Superbrands Council 2015. In addition, Jennifer is a member of the EMEA board of the Entrepreneurs' Organization. She is an advisory board member for sustainability consulting start-up Vertigo Ventures and a mentor at start-up incubator Seedcamp.

Having spent her formative childhood years in the country, Jennifer is a trustee of a South African charity called Afrika Tikkun, keeping her South African roots close to her heart.

A mother to three children, she is still searching for that elusive work-life balance!

ACKNOWLEDGEMENTS

I'm not sure that I knew what I was taking on when I decided to write this book. But I do know that it would never have come to fruition if it weren't for the incredible input and support from those around me. From the initial seed of an idea planted by my mentor, Philip Blackwell, and the amazing generosity of all my contacts who offered interviews and introductions, to the skilful craftsmanship of Ken Langdon as my writing partner, I am truly grateful.

It's easy to get complacent when you've worked in a field for many years. And one of the greatest gifts this book has given me is that through the process of researching and writing it, I have fallen in love with my industry again. To be trusted with a company's greatest asset – its reputation – is a real privilege. And for that I'd like to thank our clients, past, present and future.

The team at Six Degrees has been unwavering in its support, despite the fact that writing has often taken me away from important work I could have been doing with them. Yet, in asking them to step up, each and every one of the team has demonstrated capabilities way beyond what was expected of them. A particular thank you to Kaylin Duckitt, who helped create the space for me to write, and stepped naturally and enthusiastically into the role of chief cheerleader.

Thank you to Myles and the team at Harriman House for your patience and steady guidance, and particularly to my editor, Craig Pearce... you were right.

And finally, to my family, who have never questioned my ability to complete this project (even when I did) and have made room in our already hectic lives to make it happen. My parents and sisters have spent endless hours listening to updates, testing theories and reviewing drafts. Bethan and Izzie have coped admirably with the book taking priority above all else. Mark's calm demeanour, unconditional support, and willingness to run our life outside writing and work have kept me sane.

And to my darling PJ, I hope that in the years to come you will forgive my crazy juggling act in these early years of your life, and embrace the happiness and fulfilment that comes from truly loving your work. I dedicate this book to you.

Introduction

We are living in a time when traditional business models – and entire markets – are being disrupted at incredible speed. Rules are changing. Expectations are changing. And businesses are having to work harder than ever before to acquire and keep their customers. But what hasn't changed is the importance of your business's reputation in the race to win.

I decided to write this book for two reasons. The first is because I was regularly encountering senior communications people who understood the impact of social media on their company's reputation, but simply couldn't get buy-in internally to do anything about it. I wanted to help.

The second is because I was also encountering CEOs who felt that their grip on social media was under control because they had an intern managing a Twitter feed. And I disagreed.

I wanted to create something that took a strategic look at the impact of social media on a business's reputation… any business, big or small, selling to businesses or consumers.

There's a lot out there about the importance of business reputation and there are countless very good books on how to use social media to the benefit of your business. But I struggled to find anything that pulled all the expertise together in one place and offered a framework for solid reputation building that started with the CEO. Something that acknowledged the role social media has to play in reputation-building, but also acknowledged that it might not be right for every business, and suggested approaches businesses might take too.

Over the course of writing this book I've talked to traditional PR experts, digital gurus, drawn on my own experience in the communications industry, interviewed CEOs from businesses that handle their reputation well and not so well, and even spoken to someone whose personal reputation was tarnished beyond measure following a high-profile conviction for fraud. I've included their insights on the topic of reputation in general and social media specifically. I've also included case studies that might challenge your thinking about the role social media can play in a business.

My goal is to encourage you to think differently about your reputation. To forget old-school broadcast models and recognise today's all-communicating world for what it is: an opportunity to help shape what people think of you, to the benefit of your business.

I have not provided all the answers to the issues that social media and its impact on reputation raises. But I have included lots of questions that you may not have thought to ask. Questions to ask of yourself, your board and your teams. The end of almost every chapter includes the key questions you must ask of yourself and your organisation to address issues covered throughout that chapter.

The Reputation Playbook is broken into four sections. The first looks at the rise of corporate reputation, exploring issues like reputational risk and how to begin to get yourself in the right mindset to lead a reputation-driven business.

Section Two explores how you hardwire core values (the starting point for a solid reputation) into your business's DNA. What role does culture have to play? How can you make the most of millennials, currently the largest influx into the workforce? And finally, there's insight into the role that both company-wide and individual behaviour has in shaping your reputation.

Section Three starts to get into the practicalities of creating a reputation strategy, looking at everything from your target audience's and company's personality and tone of voice, to how to handle a crisis situation. It is by far the meatiest of the sections and includes a solid framework to work through with your senior team.

And finally, Section Four covers the justification for spending money on reputation-enhancing activities. It includes an overview of current thinking around reputation measurement and also offers a very practical approach that you can take to measurement using nothing more than your own people's time.

Having read this book I don't think you will be able to help yourself from looking at your business through a different lens. You will consider the implications on your reputation of every decision you are asked to make. You will ask challenging questions of those around you, to better understand how your reputation is treated today. You will notice the way in which you (and your customers) are greeted when they enter your office or call your business. You will spot interesting discussions on LinkedIn that you feel compelled to respond to. You may pay more attention to the way employees present themselves on social platforms.

The great news is that you will become acutely aware of your reputation and that is the starting point to building upon it. That is the gold dust which has the potential to help you leapfrog competitors and leave them wondering "How did that happen?"

I'm often asked if there is a formula for creating a great reputation and after many hours of interviews, discussions and reflection, I have come to the conclusion that I believe there is:

$$(purpose + values) \times behaviour + communications = reputation$$

There it is, a summary of the book in a tweet. And if there is one thing you take away, it ought to be acknowledgement that behaviour is the great multiplier.

I hope you enjoy *The Playbook*, but more importantly, I hope at times you feel a little uncomfortable as you read it, and are compelled to make even just a small change that will help your business grow to not only be a bigger business, but also a better business.

The Rise Of Corporate Reputation

The issue of corporate reputation is not new. As long as there have been businesses, reputation has mattered, whether it was openly addressed or not. Your business's reputation is the often intangible thing that drives people to buy from you or to want to work for you. It spurs customers to recommend you, without prompting. And it is ultimately the essence of who you are and what your business does. But what is new is how a business's reputation is affected (for good or bad) – this has changed dramatically with the advent of social media, such that it is now more of a day-to-day concern for those running businesses than it ever has been before.

Strong reputation adds brilliance to the brand

"A game-change in branding and corporate reputation is well underway. In this fast-moving information age, consumers can now readily connect the dots between the brand they buy and the company behind the brand. Whereas it has long been known that a strong brand shines a light on a company's reputation, it is now clear beyond a shadow of a doubt that a strong company reputation adds an undeniable brilliance to the brand."

Leslie Gaines-Ross, Chief Reputation Strategist, Weber Shandwick

---

Section One looks at the ways in which corporate reputation can be defined and explores why it now tops the list of issues keeping CEOs awake at night. It explores issues around reputational risk and opportunity and starts to explore how you can take the lead in establishing reputation as a business issue to be taken seriously within your company. Underpinning each of these areas are questions you should be asking of both yourself and the team you have built around you – I will draw attention to these as we go.

CHAPTER 1

Redefining
Corporate
Reputation

WHAT IS CORPORATE
REPUTATION?

When your business has a great reputation, you know it. But it is decidedly difficult to define exactly what reputation is. Some people believe it is a measure of trust. Others believe it relates to customers' willingness to recommend a company. For some it is down to the satisfaction levels of employees. Or maybe it is simply financial success. I believe it is all those things and more. A great reputation is that intangible thing that lets you know you are doing everything right.

When your business has a good reputation you have happy employees and even happier customers. You see problems as opportunities to create new customers. You are able to draw on the reserves of goodwill among those who believe in your business when you encounter tough times (as all businesses do at some point). A good reputation is a precious thing and takes time to build.

Conversely, when a good reputation is lacking, there is a tangible impact throughout the organisation. Employees are unhappy and unproductive, complaints are rife among staff and customers, and the media may repeatedly refer to the business as "troubled company, xyz".

Your company's reputation is a key asset and, just like any other asset, you must protect it from harm on the one hand and expect it to produce a return on the other. To enable you to do this, you must define what reputation means to you and your business. Where is your centre of reputational gravity?

In this book I will challenge you to think about what you are doing to enhance your business's reputation on every level and make suggestions for how to improve it.

"To illustrate the power of reputation, we can look as far back as the 1970s, to the Swiss company Nestlé. Some organisations and people objected to what they called the 'aggressive marketing' of breast milk substitutes, particularly to poor countries. A world authority then produced a code of practice on the topic, which Nestlé agreed to abide by. Nestlé and many other organisations say they work within the code; some people allege they don't. What are we to make of it? Without carrying out large-scale research to find out the details of the pros and cons, we probably go by Nestlé's reputation. A believer will simply say, 'I trust that company; so I believe they're working within the rules.'"

Richard Humphreys, former President of Saatchi & Saatchi Worldwide

ENTER
SOCIAL MEDIA

In today's world, reputation can be irreparably damaged in a matter of hours, or even minutes, as a direct result of the dramatic increase in the use of social media. This affects every single business. I have met many CEOs of large business-to-business companies who genuinely believe that social media is a consumer-driven game and really has no major impact on them. I believe that view is fundamentally flawed and in this book I will tell you why (and what to do about it).

A decade ago one unhappy customer might have told ten people about their negative experience with your brand. Even if each of those ten told another ten, you'd still be looking at hundreds, not thousands, of people hearing something negative about you. Not ideal, but not likely to affect your share price, the view of your investors or your customers' perception of the brand.

Today, using social media, one unhappy customer can tell tens of thousands of people in an instant about their poor experience with your company. And if only a fraction of those people tell someone else via social channels, the tens of thousands could turn to hundreds of thousands, or even millions... within *hours*.

OK, you might say that the people hearing these things aren't necessarily customers, so they don't really matter. You might be right. But one of the most prolific user groups on social media is journalists and they have to fill white space every day. Journalists use social media channels to look for stories that have broad appeal. It's easy to see if a random complaint by one person is echoed by hundreds or thousands. And if it is, it is easy for a journalist to dig deeper, to find out more. Unhappy or disgruntled customers love nothing more than an opportunity to tell their story.

"I can only assume that the steady increase in media outlets and access through the Internet to news as it broke had an amplifying effect."

Conrad Black, author, columnist and former publisher on the impact of social media on the most recent coverage of his legal case

And it's not just journalists using social media in clever ways to monitor businesses' reputations. Investors and financial analysts are monitoring this closely too.

In my discussion with Simon Clark, managing partner of Fidelity Growth Partners Europe, he made an interesting point:

"Today, corporate reputation has become a source of competitive advantage and a top business priority for senior executives all over the world. Investors are now looking for evidence that companies take their reputation seriously and have a measureable plan for protecting and exploiting it."

As a well-respected investor who sees hundreds of companies

a year, and analyses which will perform best in the future, he should know what he is talking about. Indeed, some experts suggest that a company's reputation can account for up to 30% (or more) of the company's value. If investors are attributing value to businesses' management of their reputations it shows business leaders need to be taking reputation seriously.

Much of the chatter on various social platforms might seem harmless – and in many cases it is. But combined with offline perceptions of your company and your brand, the conversations being held on social media have enormous power to influence your corporate reputation.

The financial impact of social media

Those sceptics who still believe social media can't really make a difference to the thing that ultimately matters most (your company's financial value) should take note:

At 2:30pm on August 13, 2013, activist investor Carl Icahn tweeted that he had invested in Apple and believed the company to be undervalued. He also hinted at positive news to follow. By 4.30pm the stock had risen to US$490. That represented an increase of US$17bn in the company's market capitalisation. It doesn't get more real than that.

BUSINESS IN THE 21ST CENTURY

Business leaders today recognise that it is a positive if their company is perceived to be doing the 'right thing' within their industry. I'm not sure if this is an evolution in collective thinking or merely the fact that as individuals have become more vocal about what matters to them via social media, companies have had to sit up and take notice.

Making money is of course the main goal for a commercial enterprise, but there are different ways to get to that end goal. Whether we're talking about a global multinational like Unilever driving profitable sustainability (at times to the detriment of profit), a small business challenging existing business models, or a venture fund with investment criteria built around workplace culture, people's perceptions of the world are changing. In order to adapt, survive and thrive, businesses need to shift their focus towards what I refer to as their reputational core.

This isn't about trends in social media; this is about the new reality of business in the 21st century. Companies with strong reputations prosper. And I believe passionately that it is possible to build a bigger business by *being* a better business, in everything you do.

Research shows that if you are unfortunate enough to suffer a blow to your reputation, the time required to fully recover could be more than three years. So, unless a business takes its guardianship of reputation very seriously, it runs the risk of suffering possibly cataclysmic damage. It will also be missing an opportunity to exploit its burgeoning reputation in order to build revenue and profits.

> "When it comes to business reputation, the greatest contributor is the combination of commercial success not marred by substantial ethical problems. It's comparatively easy to measure how people perform – if they put up the numbers, raise the equity for the shareholders and have a reputation for making a quality product and setting it up in an innovative way, that will give them the reputation. But to retain it, they have to make sure that there isn't a great ethical cloud over them."
>
> **Conrad Black**

Business is built on reputation. Reputation is driven by company behaviour. Company behaviour is amplified by social media. Understanding social media's role is critical.

There's more to this than an increase in social media activity, the importance of engagement with the community (of customers and the wider world) around your business and the potential impact of negative commentary on a brand. A focus on reputation must touch every area of your business, from HR to customer service.

REPUTATION IS NOT A COMMUNICATIONS ISSUE

Many people associate reputation with awareness and so it's often tempting to think of reputation as a communications issue, best handled by the PR team. In reality, reputation is a fundamental business issue that is at the heart of everything a company does. You build your reputation by ensuring your employees, and company as a whole, behave in line with your core values, and that you set up your systems and processes to do the same.

According to Helena Norrman, Senior Vice President of Communications at Ericsson:

"The CEO must absolutely be on board with – and drive – the reputation management process. The risks to the business become much more substantial if you say you care and take responsibility, but then don't act in a way that supports that message, as a company. Sure there's compliance in place to help govern behaviour, but in many cases acting in line with compliance requirements is black and white. It's where there are gray areas that it becomes even more critical that the company takes a stance and does the 'right' thing. The CEO and all his or her senior managers need to be prepared to act in line with the desired reputation. Sometimes that means turning deals down and making uncomfortable decisions about letting people go."

That's easier said than done. Pick any process in your company, from the speed at which you pay your suppliers to your customer service activities, and ask yourself if these are 100% aligned with what your business says is important (your core values).

It is only when you and your senior business leaders accept this new way of thinking that behaviour will change throughout a company. That behaviour change not only protects and promotes the business's reputation but also has the potential to improve the bottom line.

I will help you appreciate why leaving social media management solely to the communications teams is risky, and why a strategy built solely on the basis of what's possible with the social media platforms that exist today is extremely shortsighted.

WHY CAN'T I LEAVE IT TO THE EXPERTS?

Many books highlight the importance of understanding and evaluating the impact that today's social media channels (Google+, Facebook, YouTube, Twitter, LinkedIn and others) will have on your brand. They focus on best practice and offer advice to generate wildly successful social media campaigns. But what they don't do is explain why the CEO of a big business should care.

CEOs might not have time to read about likes, tweets and the return on investment of each social media campaign. But you do need to be asking the right questions of the right people within the business to ensure that the impact of social media on overall business reputation is fully understood and embraced.

This book combines expert knowledge with active processes to give you a framework for taking a strategic look at the role social channels can play within broader reputation management. It looks at what a company needs to do to exploit its reputation (sometimes using social media) and to protect itself from the mayhem that adverse social media activity can cause.

In the digital economy, protecting your reputation is a daily challenge.

ASK YOURSELF...

1. Do we have board-level agreement on the top three key elements that contribute to our company's reputation?

2. Do all of our processes align with our core values?

3. At the very least, do we track what important journalists are saying about us online? And the same with financial analysts?

CHAPTER 2

Reputational Risk and Opportunity

UNDERSTANDING
REPUTATIONAL RISK

The term *reputational risk* has been gaining prominence in boardrooms around the world. With the advent of social media as a catalyst, reputational risk has very quickly taken its rightful place near the top of the list of challenges that businesses face today.

According to a global survey undertaken by Deloitte Touche Tohmatsu Limited (Deloitte Global) in 2013, reputational risk was the top strategic risk faced by CEOs (up from third on the list in 2010). Henry Ristuccia, Deloitte Global Leader for Governance, Risk and Compliance explains,

> "The rise of reputation as the prime strategic risk is a natural reaction to recent high-profile reputational crises, as well as the speed of digital and social media and the potential loss of control that accompanies it."

Reputational risk is closely linked with other hot topics such as governance, sustainability, ethical business and integrity. But among these business buzzwords, reputational risk stands out because it is owned and controlled to a large extent by your stakeholders. With governance, *you* control whether or not you measure up; with sustainability, *you* control whether your business meets or exceeds important, globally-agreed metrics. You can most certainly take action to influence reputation, but you cannot directly control what people think of you.

So what is reputational risk?

Reputational risk is the potential impact on your business's reputation from both internal and external sources. It is a measure of how a company's reputation can be irreparably damaged by a single action or decision by almost anyone in the business, or anyone outside the business.

The situation is dramatically different from a decade ago when there were no global social media platforms to enable the transparency that exists today. Ten years ago, if a junior employee made an inappropriate comment to a customer the business would no doubt have taken action to discipline the employee and put things right with the customer. The situation was manageable and broad reputational risk was low.

Today, however, that same scenario can easily take place on social media channels in the public eye, with everyone able to share widely with a single click. The broad reputational risk is extremely high. It is now easy for issues as wide-ranging as product and service quality, governmental, environmental and regulatory compliance, working conditions, human rights and supply chain problems to come to the fore in a very public way.

Deloitte: exploring strategic risk

The rise of social media, which enables instantaneous global communications, is making it harder for companies to control how they are perceived in the marketplace. Findings from 300 executives surveyed by Deloitte showed that the majority believe that social media has transformed reputation management and nearly 50% cited social media as a potential industry disrupter above other contenders such as analytics, mobile applications and cyber attacks. The report by Deloitte said:

"Reputation is now rated as the highest impact risk area – not just overall, but for most individual sectors as well. Three years ago, reputation was already the top risk area in financial services – and remains so today. However, in the energy sector, for example, reputation risk wasn't even in the top five three years ago, but today is number one – perhaps fuelled by headlines about fracking, oil spills, pipeline leaks and the Alberta 'tar' sands. A similar rise in reputation risk has occurred in life sciences and healthcare, likely driven by healthcare reform efforts in the US and ongoing concerns about the skyrocketing cost of pharmaceuticals and health services."

In fact, as a result of its importance, reputational risk was addressed at the 2013 World Economic Forum (WEF) in Davos. After interviewing 1,000 industry leaders and risk experts, WEF issued the *Insight Report Global Risks Eighth Edition*, stating that the spread of false information across the web ranks alongside economic failures, environmental dangers and disease, among others, as one of today's top global threats. The report talked of "digital wildfires in a hyper-connected world" and warned of the chaos that rapidly spread misinformation and malicious information could cause in the world.

Social media activity can be harmful to business

On a UK public holiday in August 2012 an Odeon cinema customer vented his anger at a disappointing cinema experience and the post now has more than 25,000 comments and 297,000 likes on the official Odeon Facebook page. It looks as though the cinema chain had no systems in place to nip such a complaint in the bud quickly and there were inadequate processes in place to allow the company to respond to experiences that didn't live up to its mission to 'passionately deliver an exceptional entertainment experience to our guests'.

It is clear that Odeon did eventually respond to the customer, and while the damage limitation it exercised was too little and came too late, it seems that the topic is such an emotive one that Odeon had little power to stop the firestorm once it had begun to spread. Naturally, Odeon is reluctant to publish the financial damage this single failure caused; but going by the huge response, it could have been substantial.

MITIGATING
REPUTATIONAL RISK

Risk management means different things to different businesses. In banking and insurance, risk management is primarily a financial process for measuring (and hopefully managing) exposure. To the manager of a nuclear power plant, risk management is all about avoiding physical disaster and perhaps involves community relations. Only you can identify where the most fundamental risks to your reputation lie.

Since reputational risk is effectively controlled by the perception of stakeholders, the smartest approach is to make a plan to handle it and mitigate it in a controlled way. In most businesses, this comes down to management by the public relations team.

However, reputation, and therefore PR's impact on it, is an integral part of broader business success. This evolution of reputation into a boardroom issue pulls some traditional public relations people out of their natural communications comfort zone. In my experience, PR people generally lack the confidence of other professionals, like management consultants and lawyers, to tackle boardroom issues and board members. It is important that you create a channel directly from the communications teams, who are acting as the eyes and ears of the business, into the boardroom.

Good mitigation starts from being well prepared. The only real way to mitigate reputational risk is to know what's going on as early as possible. That means monitoring and listening to what the on and offline world has to say, analysing the data and watching for trends.

This is not to say that mitigating the risk of reputation damage is just about media monitoring. Perhaps most important, it's about gaining deep knowledge about customer satisfaction, employee feedback, complaints and competitors, and taking preemptive action.

There's lots of talk about social media analytics in many large companies but this information is rarely used beyond the marketing team. It reaches the customer service team if you're really lucky, but potentially critical data is not being shared or used within the wider business. It isn't getting to the board, which is where it needs to be. If this sounds like your business, the situation needs to change.

The solution, I believe, is to build a behaviour-focused business, with a clear view of what the company wants to be known for. And then make sure this behaviour is understood (and embraced) at every level in the business.

Unilever is an example of a company that I believe is doing a good job of mitigating reputational risk by focusing on ensuring that its behaviour is aligned with its values. According to the *Daily Telegraph*, Unilever chief executive Paul Polman plans to double the company's turnover while halving its environmental impact. His company is home to some of the biggest global brands – from Dove soap and Ben & Jerry's ice cream to PG Tips and Pot Noodle. The *Telegraph* reported:

> "Polman is not content with being chief shelf-stacker to the world's retailers. He wants his company to be loved. He wants to transform corporations such as his from the Aunt Sallies of environmental and social campaigners – from being the bad guys who run sweatshops and ransack the rainforests – into good guys who improve both working conditions and the environment. And he believes there is money in this altruism."

Armed with such a clear corporate sense of purpose, the Unilever PR department is equipped to produce a reputation strategy (and a social media plan) to genuinely reflect the business' goals. Empowering your PR department, and indeed the whole business, in this way – by having a clear sense of purpose in what you do – is the first step towards mitigating reputational risk, as will become increasingly clear throughout the book.

You can only make this reputation-focused shift happen by appointing a senior member of staff in a cross-functional role to be accountable for it. Someone who can pull information in from customer services, the legal team, HR and even IT, and then report this back to the boardroom. The business functions involved will depend very much on your own business – the areas that affect your stakeholders most directly are the areas to which you need to be paying closest attention. It's not a question of adding paperwork and reporting mechanisms to another function in the business; it's a case of someone picking up and coordinating what is already there.

PR departments need to understand that their role has changed too. Traditionally they would expect to be regularly challenged to prove that the work they are doing is delivering benefits and would often resort to furious action as quickly as possible to prove they were busy doing things.

However, as we discussed in Chapter 1, it's important to remember that once the company's purpose and core values are agreed, it is its *behaviour* that is the great multiplier. Good communication can help fan the flames of the spark that consistent, positive behaviour creates. Only once a business knows what its desired reputation is, and can back that up with solid, indisputable proof points, can great communication add value to the mix. If PR continues to fire from the hip, pumping out messages that are inconsistent with how the organisation actually presents itself to its stakeholders, there is a high risk that this PR work is irrelevant and the spend a waste of money. Worse, the reputational risk increases.

As part of this process, you need to ask your PR people the tough questions:

- Do we genuinely know what our customers, employees and suppliers think of us? If not, why not?

- What are we doing to influence their perception? Is it working? And how do we know?

- Do we get regular updates and insights from every functional area of the business (not just product/business units but HR, legal and IT teams)? Does this shape what we say and how we communicate?

- Can you show me examples?

- Are we prepared for the unexpected? What's the plan for dealing with the sorts of things that could spark a negative 'digital wildfire'?

- Are we clear about *why* we are communicating? What is our greater purpose as a business, and does the content and way that we communicate reflect that?

- What is the process for gauging the risk to our reputation that a particularly negative article in the media or conversation online might have?

WORKING WITH THE CHIEF RISK OFFICER

A change in mindset must be supported by operational structures. In many cases this will mean elevating the role of the public relations team (beyond 'just communications') and acknowledging the importance of reputation in other business functions.

In many businesses today, reputational risk may naturally fall under the responsibility of the Chief Risk Officer (CRO). The CRO is the executive accountable for the efficient and effective management of significant opportunities and risks in a business. Typically the CRO might categorise risks as strategic, operational, financial or compliance-related.

CROs are accountable to the executive committee and the board for reviewing factors that could negatively affect investments or a company's business interests. Most CEOs would expect their CRO to help the business balance risk and reward. In a simplified explanation, the CRO advises on increasing risk for increased return, then the board decides whether to take the risk or not.

What's your business-killer?

According to Rivo CEO, Steve Husk, "Every company's reputation is under threat from something, somewhere, at pretty much any given time. It's a matter of what is relevant right now to their customers and the public. There are threats that are always relevant and high impact such as fatalities or mass injury – but increasingly threat is also about what is socially acceptable, which is changing in terms of where the bar is set and how quickly people know about events. Reputational risk is no longer about just what is relevant to the core business in hand. If you are a clothing manufacturer and your offshore factory collapses, that's equally bad news as being a clothing retailer and being highlighted as a FTSE 100 paying incredibly low corporation taxes. It's irrelevant really whether it's about the clothing or not – it's about what we tolerate as acceptable business behaviour as a society, as well as a paying customer or shareholder."

Adding reputation to the CRO's list of risk types sort of makes sense, but in my opinion it is a rather defensive strategy and doesn't take into account the potential opportunity created by identifying reputational risks on the horizon.

Let's consider one example. In Europe there is much debate about the high roaming fees charged by mobile network operators when subscribers are travelling outside their home country. This creates bad feeling among customers and fairly regularly results in negative media coverage when stories emerge of unexpectedly high phone bills being received on returning home. It is, without doubt, a reputational issue faced by many mobile operators. But perhaps more significantly, it means most customers limit their mobile phone (and specifically mobile data) use while travelling abroad, so reducing the potential revenue anyway. The European Commission is currently talking about abolishing roaming charges altogether, which will inevitably have a significant impact on operator revenue over the medium to long term.

Commercially, one might think that it makes sense for a network operator to continue to get as much revenue as it can for as long as it can, specifically the incumbents who have the most to lose. And a CRO may well be involved in the strategic discussions on the subject of pricing and roaming legislation. But challenger brands have clearly identified a (potentially purpose-driven?) opportunity to take a longer-term view, turning reputational risk into commercial opportunity. Offering very simple roaming options, with no catch, before they are forced to do so by a regulatory body inevitably builds up goodwill among customers, encouraging them to recommend the service and ultimately stay loyal to the operator.

Put someone in charge of reputation

"Having a solid reputation boils down to expectations. Are the business' products and services delivering what is expected of them? If not, you leave people feeling like they're getting ripped off and that's never a good thing. Reputation is a function of something, so ultimately you need someone responsible for making sure those functions are taking place. I have a formula that I use for turning failing businesses around – communications is an important part of it. And with the businesses I work with, it is increasingly important to look at the risk profile when it comes to reputation. It is critical to stay on top of what's being said about your company, customers, competitors and your market."

Michael Jalbert, former CEO, EF Johnson

Essentially, a CRO's role is to warn the company that it is about to go over a cliff while there is still time to change direction. If reputational risk management is owned by the CRO, the handling of any real risk-related issues that arise often falls between the cracks. The CRO has his or her own set of tools and processes to measure and monitor risk, but when a risk becomes a reality, the people involved in the risk project will handle the physical outcome – so who handles the reputation outcome? Handing it to the communications team at the eleventh hour isn't the most effective way to get a positive outcome for your reputation.

I believe that if you create an opportunity for the CRO to have a sparring partner, in the form of a Chief Reputation Officer, the conversations will ultimately lead to a more sustainable win for the business. In other words, approaching reputational risk in the right way allows you to transform it from a risk into an opportunity.

THE CHIEF REPUTATION OFFICER

The individual who adopts the role of Chief Reputation Officer (in description, if not title) should work closely with the risk expert to monitor and track risk. They must also work closely with HR executives – because ultimately every risk relates to people in some way. The Chief Reputation Officer must of course also be directly linked to the communications/PR team.

The person will have strong business and analytical skills, coupled with excellent communications skills and the ability to make decisions fast; to begin with, at least half of their time will be in fire-fighting mode.

There will likely be some tricky decisions about reporting structures. The role is cross-functional so the best route is probably to agree that each business division appoints a full or part-time executive responsible to the Chief Reputation Officer on a dotted-line basis. It is almost certain that the Chief Reputation Officer's power within the organisation will depend on their charisma and ability to motivate people. You can't simply force people into exhibiting a company's core beliefs.

As their influence increases and the positive and active side of reputation management takes hold, the Chief Reputation Officer will spend more time in planning and encouraging mode.

Ultimately the organisation will realise that its reputation is its most valuable asset and that the role of protecting and exploiting it is crucial. By that time, the Chief Reputation Officer will have become the CEO's right-hand man or woman.

Pick a strong candidate for the role

The Chief Reputation Officer you choose should command immediate respect from business managers and their people. It will be seen as an operational role and if there is any possibility that the team could see this new person as having failed in their last job they are dead in the water. It's hard to pull such a strong manager out of their current job but, as we've already seen, reputation is key in the social media-driven world.

- What do you think is the greatest risk to our reputation, both online and offline?

- Do we have a clear view of where the reputational risk for our company lies?

- What's our business-killer?

- Do we have a plan for mitigating reputational risk? And who is accountable for it?

- Are we integrating our own communications experts at board level?

- Are we looking to create an opportunity out of reputational risk?

- Who would be a natural leader in the Chief Reputation Officer role?

CHAPTER 3

It Starts
With You

QUESTIONS EVERY CEO
NEEDS TO ASK

How can you turn this theory about purpose, values and behaviour into reality for your business? And how can you be sure it will drive your business' reputation in a positive direction?

There are, I'm afraid, no guarantees that putting money and top notch resources into reputation and social media planning will bring a satisfactory return. So much of your success will depend on decisions made in the moment. Using the framework in this book will reduce the risks, but ignoring the impact that social media has on reputation is simply not an option.

The most important questions business leaders need to ask are these:

- Is our business reputation a priority? Is it addressed at board level? If not, why not?

- Are we genuinely using social media and the data available as a result of it to our advantage?

- As a business leader, could I personally be doing more on social media? And if I did, does it have the potential to enhance our business reputation?

- Do I have someone I trust taking responsibility for activities in this area and reporting back to me?

WHAT'S YOUR ROLE AT THE
FRONT LINE?

Are you and your senior team going to become contributors to one or more of the main social media platforms? There are good reasons to do so, but there are risks involved as well.

Plunging in at the deep end and getting involved personally in social media warrants careful thought.

If you are planning your first foray into social media, there is a LinkedIn ranking that offers a kind of benchmark and a reasonable set of objectives. LinkedIn runs a regular ranking of the world's top CEOs with a presence on social media. The way they do the ranking uses Klout as a starting point. Klout may not be the most robust measure, but it is a consistent one. It is a ranking based on the influence you exert in social media. It counts the number of times people have responded to a blog, tweet or other social media contribution you have made. LinkedIn regards this score as quantitative and a bit 'raw'. It looks at added value. In terms of its own rankings, LinkedIn says:

> "[CEOs'] value added was measured in terms of originality and positive impact on the corporate world, their industry, and application to their own company. We favored CEOs who had actively contributed to the leadership agenda. We reduced their score if it was seen as too obviously self-promoting or if we believe they have no direct involvement in social media content. We favored CEOs who had consistently contributed over time."

The latest findings show that the list of the top ten most social CEOs is not made up only of consumer brands. Not surprisingly, perhaps, Richard Branson sits at number one, but also included are Elon Musk of Tesla Motors, Jeff Immelt, CEO of GE, and Marissa Meyer, CEO of Yahoo.

Looking at the most recent top 60 list, I wondered if I could link any movement in the position of people on the list with their company's reputation. Certainly one stood out: Rupert Murdoch, whose company News International has suffered much damage to its reputation recently, is down 5 places to 13 on the LinkedIn list – just a thought.

Being active on social media doesn't mean posting pictures of what you've had for dinner. It's an opportunity for you to share your passion for the field you are in, and to have direct access to the stakeholders who are important to you. How can that NOT be a good thing? But take care – getting involved must be driven by a genuine desire to do so, not because your PR team tells you it's a good way to broadcast news. Go into it with your eyes wide open.

Looking at today's social media landscape, I would suggest that LinkedIn and Twitter are the best places for a CEO to start. LinkedIn has evolved to be a useful platform to share deep insight and opinions on topical issues. It has an 'influencer' programme which showcases inspirational and insightful blog posts from luminaries ranging from Bill Gates to President Barack Obama. This allows selected thought-leaders (their term) to share original content directly with LinkedIn users.

According to Dharmesh Shah, entrepreneur, investor and founder of Hubspot:

> "In less than a year the Influencer program has become an incredibly powerful platform. There are now over 300 Influencers including people like NYC Mayor Michael Bloomberg, HP CEO Meg Whitman, Zappos CEO Tony Hsieh, journalist Maria Shriver, UK Prime Minister David Cameron … and the list goes on. The average Influencer post receives almost 30k views. (Some receive over a million views, with the top post receiving almost 2m views.) The audience is extremely diverse: 22 percent of Influencer followers are entry-level professionals while 49 percent are director-level and above."

Following these influencers will not only give you their insights into improving your business, but you also have the possibility of posting yourself.

This is the current list of influencers, but LinkedIn is in the process of opening up its blogging platform to all of its users: **www.linkedin.com/today/influencers**

If blogging is a step beyond where you wish to go, even simply sharing links to content you have created via your LinkedIn profile means you are tapping into an existing and very well-respected platform to get your opinions heard.

And there are good reasons to be on Twitter as well. There can be no better way to find people with the same interests and engage in conversations with them. Or simply to listen. That might be to a customer group, where you can get direct feedback on just about anything. Or maybe it is up-to-the-minute updates on emerging issues or crises around the world.

True, putting your head above the parapet on any form of social media is not without its risks, and there will certainly be days when you wonder why you did it. But if you take your reputation seriously, you won't have to look very hard for the answer to the question, "Do I take the plunge, or not?"

Many CEOs have decided not to be involved directly, even though people within their companies may well be avid users of all the social media channels. It takes time out of a busy diary. You could make a simple mistake, even just a typo, and end up with bad news for you and your organisation going viral. The excuses are endless.

However, there is good reason to consider the opposite argument. Former Medtronic Inc CEO Bill George, a management professor at Harvard Business School and avid tweeter, put it quite succinctly in an article in *Barron's*: "People want CEOs who are real. They want to know what you think," he says, adding: "Can you think of a more cost-effective way of getting to your customers and employees?"

There is a trend for CEOs to be on Twitter with others tweeting on their behalf. I'd rather see a CEO tweet less frequently and know it was him or her than see multiple tweets a day and know it was someone hired to do the job for them, but which way you go about it is up to you.

A SIMPLE STARTING POINT

I believe it's impossible to understand the power of social media until you have experienced it. So get yourself involved in some way, whether it is through a personal or business profile. But a word of warning, if you decide to go down the personal route, for example by setting up a Facebook page, make sure your security settings are properly configured.

Watch how you behave

"Business reputation is won by performance. Not only by how the company's products perform, but by how its people behave, especially the CEO. And that performance is easier to see and easier to share now than it ever has been before, whether it is via email, online forums or on social media sites. As a journalist, Facebook is the first place I look for sources. It's amazing how many senior executives don't bother using proper privacy settings and leave their page open for all to see!"

Fred Langan, Canadian broadcast journalist, former host CBC Business News

---

Here's an easy suggestion for some low-risk and low-commitment social media activity you can undertake personally. Assuming you already have a LinkedIn profile and if your company has a blog, why not draft an opinion piece and share it on LinkedIn?

Just see what happens. As long as the opinion is well backed up, has solid arguments and is factually correct, you have very little to lose. Take some time over your first effort.

Here's a neat way of doing it: take a current preoccupation that businesses in general have (it could be specific to your industry or something with broad appeal). Think of an angle that a typical businessperson might take in writing an opinion piece on that topic. Reject that angle because everyone will take it. Think harder to find another angle ... and reject that too – a small but significant percentage of people will take that view.

Think of one more way of looking at the problem you've identified and you have an angle that is original. Write that up (it doesn't need to be long, even 200 words will suffice) and publish it. Your first effort will be top quality. And don't forget to monitor (and respond to) any comments people might write as a result of your post. I suspect you'll find it empowering.

LEADING BY EXAMPLE

Of all the CEOs I talked to about reputation management, there's one thing they've agreed on unanimously. When asked how a business ensures that the behaviour of its people is in line with its core values, they all say that it starts with you, the business leader. You set the tone for *the way things are done around here*, which in turn reinforces the business's reputation one way or another. Undoubtedly you walk the talk on your values; social media offers you another way of reinforcing them to all your stakeholders. And remember, the more your company behaviour stays in line with your core values, the less likely you are to see a digital wildfire emerge around a crisis on social media.

Getting involved in the world of social media isn't easy. It creates issues that your business might never have had to deal with before. But I believe the best businesses are addressing it now, before they are forced by competitive as well as financial pressures to do so.

Let's take the example of an old-school manufacturing company. In my experience, senior people within such a company tend to see Facebook as a minefield, with employees all over the world posting potentially inappropriate things. Balancing that negativity is a positive force from the millennials in your business who want to feel proud of their company – and its Facebook profile is a public vehicle for that pride. They also want to be able to connect with the work community on social media. My advice to the leaders of businesses that fear the ramifications of having a Facebook page is that if you are worried about this then the problem goes much more to the fundamentals of your business. Do you have a culture where making negative, derogatory or insulting comments is OK in any forum, whether online or offline? If so, I'd suggest the problem is cultural, not a social media one.

Ultimately, it is at a business level and not at a social media level that leaders need to address their fears. Get the culture right and the risk of social media catastrophe reduces dramatically. And while you are figuring that out, get your social media monitoring in place, because 'listening' to the relevant conversations taking place should be non-negotiable.

When all is working well, you will know it, because you will feel a great energy around the business and what you do. You will sense the goodwill you and the team are building up. And you will start to see the potential that other social media platforms have to offer.

To our generation, despite the fact that email contributes substantially to information overload, it has become a critical aspect of how we communicate. For many people, if our inbox is under control, then our job is under control too.

So, it's tempting to think that using email extensively means you don't have to consider any other method of communication. You could take the view that social media is just another passing fad designed to take up time and stop you from doing real work. OK, it's not a bad idea to have that debate with yourself when you're contemplating creating personal social media profiles. But don't let your personal technology fatigue (or fear) hamper your business sense.

If the current emerging workforce hadn't been raised on technology, social media might go away. But it won't. It is in the millennials' make-up. And if you think of nothing else, think about how you propose to attract the next generation of exceptional talent if your business is hamstrung by old-fashioned thinking.

For those sceptics who are holding back, I have a question: if you could know exactly what groups of customers, suppliers or employees were feeling and saying about your business, right now, would you want to know?

I am assuming the answer is yes. That's what data from social media platforms (and all other types of communication) can give you. We talked about data earlier in the context of mitigating reputational risk. Gathering the information is one thing, analysing it properly and *acting* on the results is quite another. The ability to use this data requires fresh thinking in an organisation – a more collaborative approach.

Gathering data

If you don't have your own social profile, ask your kids if you can do a search from their Facebook page to see the number of people linked to your company. You may not be able to see what they're saying, but it will give you an idea of the scale of engagement your business is attracting. Do the same on LinkedIn. Use the search function on Twitter and YouTube to look for mentions of your company too. You might be surprised by what you see.

Don't be tempted just to 'shut it down' and refuse to allow the people who work in your company to do what comes naturally. Remember this is a generation of chronic sharers. And others may see what you might perceive as wholly inappropriate quite differently. Hopefully you will see some really positive stuff, reinforcing your core values and beliefs, and making you proud of the company you run.

If you choose to do nothing else, simply listen. The chances are your organisation already has some social media monitoring in place. So as a first step look at the headline figures. Reflect on them. Talk about them. Think about what lies behind them.

A colleague of mine recently did some research for a large global B2B brand which showed that the social media presence of the brand and its main rival was pretty similar. But she dug a little deeper and found that the nature of the social media mentions was marginally but significantly different. Although the general sentiment relating to both brands was pretty positive, the posts about the competitive brand were predominantly from employees, saying amazing things about the company they work for. The positive culture is shining through for all to see. And in my experience, happy teams mean happy customers.

I would consider going several steps beyond just social media monitoring, however. There is software available today which enables you to track and monitor all the areas of your business that contribute to your reputational risk. You can track IT-related security breaches, major health and safety incidents or the general tone of media coverage. Having the data to hand is priceless, not only to look for patterns and ultimately predict where potential problems lie, but also to reinforce any messaging if a crisis strikes. Instant information gives the power to react instantly.

A large fire and rescue service in the UK, for example, wanted to move away from its paper-based accident and near miss reporting system. It bought bespoke software, from a company called Rivo, and gained all the benefits it expected plus the bonus of a measurable improvement in the safety culture. Its people reported as near to 100% of accident and near misses as management could possibly expect. These all added to the database of information the company could use for planning purposes.

The key is to identify the most important facets of your business and then monitor them. The information exists. In most cases it's simply a matter of identifying what data to collect, putting the processes in place to collect it and then reviewing the stories it tells you.

ASK YOURSELF...

- Am I and the top management of my business going to be actively involved in social media?

- Do I really know what image of my business is being portrayed online?

- Does the board pay attention to the data coming into the company via social media?

- What issue in my industry makes me feel so passionate that I want to shout about it from the rooftops? Can I start talking about this on social media?

Hardwiring Core Values Into Business DNA

Having understood the increasing importance of corporate reputation in the social media age, the next step is to start to unpeel the layers to reveal your business's reputational core. Here we start to look in more detail at what it means to be a purpose-driven business and how you can ensure your company behaviour reinforces your desired reputation.

Section Two explores the potential that culture and behaviour have to multiply your company's purpose and values, positively contributing to reputation. We look at the role youth – and specifically the generation raised with social media – has to play in your business. And finally, this section includes a breakdown of the traditional functions within any business, the questions you could be asking of those working in these roles and what they should be asking of themselves.

Tackling cynicism from the inside

"I believe that the last three decades have seen many shifts when it comes to how brands communicate. One of the most fundamental ones is a much greater cynicism and questioning of authority among people in general. This means that today, building trust must be a top business priority. But with the ubiquity of social media, trust can so quickly and easily be destroyed. As a result, I believe the first audience any business must focus on is the internal one. They need to understand the impact that their behaviour can have on the reputation of the business."

Richard Humphreys, former President of Saatchi & Saatchi Worldwide

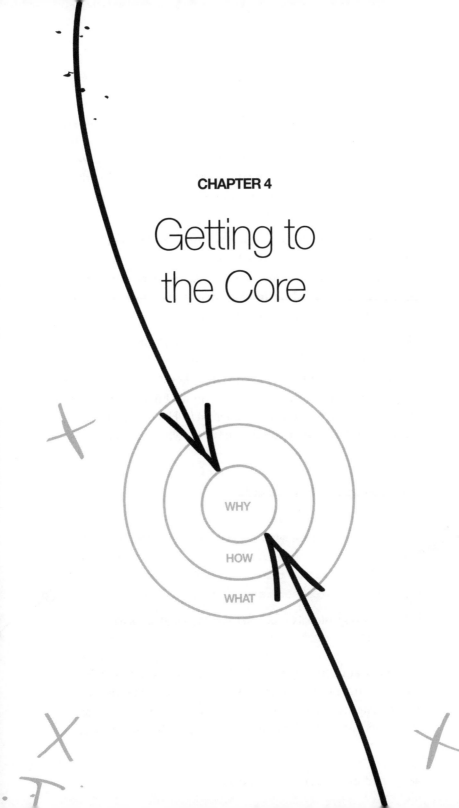

CHAPTER 4

Getting to
the Core

WHY

HOW

WHAT

We've already said that business reputation is driven primarily by your company's behaviour, which in turn is driven by a solid understanding among your people of your core values and greater purpose as a business. At the heart of this theory is the ability for a business to find and articulate its *why* (also known as its purpose or mission).

Author Simon Sinek has created a simple model to help define why some companies far outshine competitors with the same resources and in the same markets. At the core of this model is a deep understanding of what drives the business, beyond making money (which should be a given).

His proposal is that every business communicates what it does, whether this is a product or a service. Most companies communicate about how they do what they do but only the best companies communicate *why* they do it. This is a company's true purpose. He calls it the *golden circle*. His conclusion is that people don't buy what you do, they buy why you do it.

The corporate brand is the anchor

"In this always-on, multi-platform, uncertain world, corporate brands are more important than ever because they provide an anchor of trust and credibility in a sea of dynamic, continual change. A strong corporate brand is essential to unlocking the full value of the enterprise and strengthening its brands, products and services as a result."

Micho Spring, Global Corporate Chair, Weber Shandwick

Google wants to organise the world's information while at the same time doing no evil. Amazon wants to be the world's most customer-centric company. Coca-Cola strives to inspire moments of optimism and happiness. These companies give strong indicators of what drives them. In all cases, the companies concerned also have well-defined core values that underpin these statements. When it comes to reputation, the interesting part is to examine whether the companies both behave and communicate in a way that is in line with their purpose and their values. More on that later.

I believe that the companies with the strongest reputations get their *why* right. Their underlying purpose is quite clear when they do anything, whether that is to communicate, sell, buy, or hire staff.

If you want to check that your company has a clear *why* and is living up to this day-to-day, good questions to ask yourself are:

- Does your company have a purpose (beyond making money)? Why does the company do what it does?

- What is your desired reputation? What do you want to be known for? If you can't state it in a sentence, try writing down the words that you want to spring to mind when people think about your brand.

- What do you personally believe are your business's biggest strengths?

- If you had to choose just one strength, what would that be?

- Now think about how your business operates – can you list ten examples of actions (big or small) that reinforced your desired reputation in the past working week? These actions could be by you or (preferably) others in the business.

Understanding your belief set and knowing why your company exists will help you and your team make values-based decisions (no matter how big or small), which is a fundamental step in building strong foundations for a long-lasting, positive reputation. Equally, if your employees can see what the objectives of the organisation are, it is easier for them to fulfil their part in achieving those objectives, and to feel motivated in doing so.

USING REPUTATION
STRATEGY AS THE DRIVER

Defining and communicating the business's purpose and values is one thing, but getting every single employee to live and breathe them is quite another. This has always been a challenge for business leaders, but in today's always-on, all-communicating world, the issue is more acute. There is a challenge here, but the landscape also creates incredible opportunities, both to connect with people within the business and for your values-driven behaviour to shine through to your most important stakeholders. I believe the most effective way to begin to hardwire your values into the business is to create a dedicated reputation strategy.

The objective of this strategy is to ensure everyone in the organisation behaves in a way that supports your business's reason for being.

Where does it start?

There's no alternative: it starts with the CEO. It is essential for you to understand and truly believe that reputation management is critical to the business. It always has been in a sense, but social media – with its sheer scale and spread – brings reputation management to the front of the competitive battle.

Surprisingly, not all CEOs are taking social media seriously. A recent study by Edelman-owned Zeno group found that one-third of CEOs failed to consider their company's social media reputation when making business decisions. My take is that there is no such thing as a distinct social media reputation. What's said online has a significant impact on your company's overall reputation – can you afford to ignore it?

Getting buy-in

There is no point, however, in developing reputation-focused plans if people will not implement them. It's critical to get buy-in from those people in your organisation who will be responsible for making things happen. And that's pretty much everyone.

I'm not talking here about the specialist communications team. This team has probably been making presentations and encouraging better use of social media for years; it's likely bought in already. I'm talking about the 'I don't have time for Twitter' people and the 'Facebook is for my teenage children' people. Don't underestimate the number of these people, nor how deep-seated their suspicion of the new environment is. The point is that it's not their personal activity on social platforms that matters, but the fact that their interactions (with customers, suppliers, anyone really) have the potential to be openly shared on these new platforms, at the touch of a button.

There are two main issues in getting buy-in to your reputation strategy and it is worth thinking about these before creating it. The first is *resistance to change*. Where core values are poorly articulated and not transparent to your workforce and customers, or where there has been little attention paid to reputation building (or social media), overcoming resistance may involve a management programme to produce major change.

In a company that is social media savvy, proud of its core values and where people are eager to act as company ambassadors, all you have to do is guide the development of a reputational plan and make sure the organisation supports its implementation.

Where does your company lie on this spectrum?

The second difficulty is *getting people to understand what you are aiming for*. You don't necessarily want people to sign up to all-singing, all-dancing social media campaigns. It's not as simple as that. You may do those eventually, but if they're not right for your business there's no need for them. You need to be fully aware of the potential pitfalls, challenges and opportunities of social media based on real-world and online behaviour. The first step is to ensure every single action, decision or campaign is aimed at enhancing the company's overall reputation.

When considering your reputation strategy, make sure that:

- The person you hold accountable for overseeing the reputation strategy has a clear mandate from you, the CEO, to produce the strategy and, more importantly, to implement it.

- This plan cascades in an appropriate way to all levels of the business and is woven into business operations.

- Your reputation strategy truly addresses and outlines a way of behaving – not merely a list of communications tactics supporting product or service lines.

Section Three includes a detailed breakdown of what should go in your plan.

Supporting the business plan

Whether the focus is short, medium or long term, most successful businesses will have clear goals in place and an overall plan to achieve those goals. It is critical that the reputation strategy is 100% in support of that business plan – looking at behaviour throughout the organisation as well as internal and external communications. If you pay enough attention to the organisation's purpose and values, the communications part should follow quite naturally.

The starting point is to think about a reputation strategy rather than a communications strategy, so we start to shift our thinking away from the traditional silos where the implementation might ordinarily fall. This is important. It ensures that everyone in the organisation who needs to contribute to the plan gets an opportunity to do so, and it means there is the potential to make values-driven recommendations that require fundamental operational (and behavioural) changes. Passing the task straight to the PR team as a simple communication task produces a problem identified by the grandfather of public relations Harold Burson: it emphasises communications at the expense of behaviour change.

LESS CENTRALISED AND LESS REGULATED COMMUNICATIONS

Let's think more about how we move the focus away from trying to control communications and take the company's core values and its *why* – the things that form its reputation – as the starting point instead. Attempts to control the outward communications of every single person in your company's ecosystem are futile. What is more, the digital age has led to a basic change in reputation management. Where once any company communication had to be approved before it could be sent out, often by several parties, communications responsibility is now shared by company employees *en masse*.

In the past, for example, people in the organisation referred all journalist enquiries to the press office. Staff in a shop referred questions or requests made by a customer to the manager, and managers often deferred to head office over anything not concerned with the microcosm of their shop. The sheer number of people in your organisation who now interact with the general public makes that sort of thinking outdated.

In fact, many businesses today have an overt strategy that involves peer-to-peer support. Take mobile communications provider Vodafone, for example. A significant percentage of its customer enquiries are handled on a customer forum hosted by the company, where they are answered by other customers before a business representative even has the opportunity to respond.

In this age of social media, a company's actions send out as loud a message as its advertising and PR programmes. Its actions shape its reputation more than its words. What you say to your customers and prospects through advertising, PR and other promotion takes second place to the performance of your products and how you deal with customers after they have bought.

One poor response to a customer enquiry doesn't lose one sale, it potentially loses all the sales to the people who are put off by a bad review or a negative tweet from the embittered prospect. Don't forget such a response could come from anyone in the organisation without any sort of filtering. This is particularly true of a negative comment that has perhaps been made somewhere public, but not in the formal customer communications channels. All it takes is a well-intentioned employee, standing up for the company in a way that is perceived as negative or inappropriate, to spark a much wider public discussion.

These changing conditions mean that you can no longer rely on a standard holding statement in response to a tricky journalist question. That might have been acceptable in the past, but today it's not just journalists, but also customers and other stakeholders asking the tough questions – increasingly on public platforms like Facebook, LinkedIn or Twitter. This requires a human response, fast. A customer who asks a difficult question about the performance of your product is going to report back not only on what your customer service people said, but also on how your company responded, and what you did. There is an added expectation.

This is why communications in business have become less regulated and less centralised – businesses need to respond faster and with a human voice, two functions which are aided by opening communications out to a wider base of employees and allowing them to communicate without being overseen. And doing this with confidence means it is critical that every single employee understands the company's core values and behaves in line with them.

Today, customers in both B2B and B2C environments want professionalism, and they want it with a human face. A great example from the B2B world is Maersk Line. As one of the world's largest container shipping companies, it's hard to think of a more traditional industry. Recently, Maersk Line decided to use social media to contribute to its customer acquisition, but recognised from the beginning that social media is about engaging and not overt marketing.

The company has an entire website dedicated to explaining its presence on social media channels, which also offers fascinating content, including regular blog posts from the captains of its ships. Its Twitter feed is a fantastic example of a previously faceless company that now reflects the very human core values around reliability, customer care and innovation. It's worth a look at **www.maersklinesocial.com**.

A business's voice is increasingly important. It provides competitive distinction and contributes to your business's human face. Of course, it is vital that the voice you decide on directly supports the reputation you are aiming for.

SEEK TO INFLUENCE, NOT CONTROL

We can make efforts to control our outward communication and we can make sure that it aligns with our core values, but we can no longer insist that every public statement made by an employee is signed off.

Are you, as a businesses leader, happy that the now familiar descriptor 'all opinions my own' as part of a Twitter, LinkedIn, Facebook or blog biography absolves employees of the potentially negative ramifications of what they say? Are you embracing the employees who are prolific on social media and contributing in a positive way to your reputation? Could you be doing more?

The social media phenomenon forces us to trust our employees with our most precious asset – our company's reputation. If they 'own' the reputation it's essential for them to have absorbed and fully bought into the company's purpose and values. Communicating – with anyone – in line with both of these (in a way that is authentic to each individual) must become second nature.

Social media platforms are widespread, with today's employees, customers and suppliers connected 24/7. People who are media savvy are also chronic sharers; they are natural storytellers. When customers are happy and voice it, they contribute to the positive reputation of your business. When they are unhappy and share it, the reverse is true. The same goes for employees.

In neither case do you have direct control over what people say. You can only make sure that everything your company does and says influences your customers and your own employees before they make their voices public. So we go back to basics. Time and again, when I talk to CEOs, there is a familiar refrain when it comes to reputation – the best way to generate a great reputation is to make sure the core of what you do, your product and customer service, are great from the word go.

ASK YOUR EMPLOYEES...

- Do you know what our core values are?
- Do these align with your personal values?
- Where is our company behaviour out of line with those values?
- What could we do better, every day, to build a stronger reputation?

CHAPTER 5

Driving a Reputation-Aware Culture

CULTURE IS THE
TRUMP CARD

One of the longest running and most contentious topics in corporate life is culture. "Culture eats strategy for breakfast" – these are wise words from management expert Peter Drucker and this was never truer than today. Get the culture wrong and you will not successfully implement any business strategy, no matter how clever it is.

A strong culture is inextricably linked to building and maintaining a strong reputation. In many ways your reputation is the outward and visible sign of your culture. In fact, I'm not sure a company can build a sustainable reputation without a strong culture where people can identify with a purpose and core values, and adhere to them.

It's not too difficult to describe the culture you aspire to. Maybe you want to drive innovation, delight your customers, be a responsible global citizen, treat your employees with trust and respect, and so on. However, what it boils down to in reality is *the way things are done around here*.

So by all means define your culture, but then look around and see if the way things actually happen in your business is in line with the way you believe things should be done. If not, you need to pay special attention to resetting the cultural thermostat in the business. This could be no more than a refresher training programme, or it may require a major change management programme involving everyone from the top down making changes to their behaviour and interactions. Sometimes it might mean parting company with those who have a clear values clash.

The truth is, culture is directly related to core values, core values are related to company and employee behaviour, and this directly impacts reputation. Culture and reputation are mutually dependent.

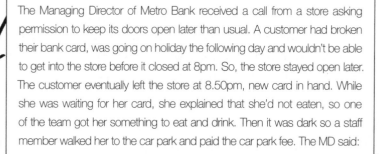

Tony Hsieh, CEO of the world's largest online shoe retailer Zappos, puts it like this:

> "Our number one priority is company culture. Our whole belief is that if you get the culture right, most of the other stuff like delivering great customer service or building a long-term enduring brand will just happen naturally on its own."

Zappos is the business most often heralded as a beacon of company culture and best practice. It holds that position for a reason. With less than 5% staff turnover and a more than 75% return customer rate, Zappos most definitely practises what it preaches.

If you've got a well-articulated and authentic purpose, and you really understand your business's *core values*, you are more than halfway there. Assuming that your core values and culture then figure prominently in your hiring practices (a very big assumption!), you should have a team that is broadly aligned. Filling your business with people who truly believe and support your purpose and values – and always act in accordance with them – is when you start to see the magic happen.

The ultimate goal, as I've said, is to ensure that every single employee understands the concept of the reputation economy and their role in contributing to the positive reputation of your business; in other words they need to walk the talk.

IT'S ACTIONS THAT MATTER, NOT WORDS

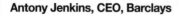

"Since we launched our purpose and values earlier this year I have been very clear that *how* we do business is as important as *what* we do. For Barclays – and indeed the banking sector – to regain the trust of stakeholders, it is going to take much more than marketing initiatives or philanthropic activities. It will take cultural change and actions rather than words."

Antony Jenkins, CEO, Barclays

No matter how many signs you have up around the office extolling your values, they are meaningless unless you empower your staff to live them.

Cameron Hulett is the Executive Director at a thriving London-based digital advertising company called Undertone. In a great example of actions building reputation, he encourages all his staff to uphold the company's values of honesty and transparency, internally and externally. When pushed on what that might look like day to day, he says, "I tell our people that the question they need to ask in any given situation is: 'What is the right thing to do?' "

Hulett cited a recent client – a major global brand with a sizeable budget – who asked one of his consultants to take a specific approach to a project. The consultant knew that it would not meet the expectations or goals of that client, so despite the fact that it meant revenue loss for the business, he turned the project down.

He talks about another example – a high-performing employee who resigned in November, one month before bonuses were due to be allocated. According to his contract, it was black and white: people who are not with the company in December do not get bonuses. But when Hullet asked himself what the right thing to do was, he felt strongly that the employee had contributed to the success of the business throughout the year and so he was awarded a substantial portion of that bonus. His other employees witnessed this action that directly supported honesty, transparency and doing the right thing.

Notably, the employee who left also did the right thing by leaving at a time that put his bonus in jeopardy. He could have waited the time out to make sure he got the bonus, even though he would have been disengaged from Undertone's business. It is actions like these that speak volumes and contribute to a positive reputation, particularly when they happen consistently over an extended period of time.

The goal in doing the right thing is to achieve the company's vision in the way its leaders aspire to. The primary goal of doing the right thing is definitely not to have people talk about it on social media. On the other hand, doing the right thing creates such a sense of goodwill that the positive sentiment shines through when people talk about the brand publicly, whether at a party, in a restaurant or on their Facebook page.

Show what your culture means through action

When you promote your culture, display it in action as well as words. By all means tell people what the aspiration is but, as Cameron Hulett suggests, articulate what it means in day-to-day situations too.

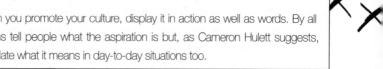

The question arises, what are you doing to empower the culture that will underpin your desired reputation? Have you made sure that your processes and rewards systems enable (or even better, encourage) your employees to work within the desired company culture? Do the pressures of everyday working life push them towards or away from the way you want them to operate?

So, if you say you are customer-focused, do your customer-facing people have the power to satisfy their customers? Have you tested this out? Phone them with a problem and see how long it is before they have to go up the line to get the answer to your query. When they come back from talking to their managers, can they completely satisfy you or is there a chance that they have to go back to their manager again? Check it out again in the not too distant future to see if the culture you define, having customer-facing people empowered to satisfy customers, remains in place.

Metro Bank offers a great example of this. There's a rule in the company for employees who get unusual questions from customers. If they must seek answers from their seniors, it takes one person to say "yes", but two to say "no". So if your boss says "yes", it stands. If your boss says "no" you must get a second opinion from another senior executive. By default, the company is encouraging yeses. That's a business that is genuinely customer focused.

Again, if you say you are focused on innovation, does the company do things aimed specifically at inspiring innovation? Innovation comes from strong leadership and recognising the best ideas. If anyone has an idea, at any level in the business, is someone listening to it? Do you have a system which encourages staff to come up with new ideas that will truly take the company forward? Does your office space inspire innovation? Do you allow employees to work from somewhere other than a fixed desk (work-permitting) from time to time? Get the answers to these questions right and you have made certain that the culture of your company is identified by actions and not words.

In the end, getting people to work within the desired culture starts and ends with leadership. Make sure that you and your senior team can never be suspected of hypocrisy. Every decision you make and every interaction you have with your people should display loudly and clearly the values that underlie your business. If you achieve this, if your people's actions are walking the talk, are you letting them know this with a big thank you?

REWARDING BEHAVIOUR

Motivation is inspiring someone to want to behave in a particular way or to passionately want to achieve something. Of course, big thank-yous by way of rewards like extra money, promotions and recognition are important in inspiring people to operate within your culture. But think about situations where you spread the word of good practice and at the same time recognise the person behind it.

What could leaders in your organisation do differently tomorrow that might help their team to feel better about themselves and inspire them to contribute even more to reputational excellence? I return to Zappos, the online shoe retailer, as a leading light for rewarding the correct behaviour.

Cultivating excellence

Inspired by Tony Hsieh, Zappos took some innovative routes to rewarding and motivating the team. The company's vision is excellence in customer service and delivering happiness. Hsieh himself says Zappos is a customer service company that just happens to sell shoes.

Some key points for the systems the company put in place include:

- Call centre staff are measured not by the usual metric of calls per minute, but by the number of unsolicited gifts they receive from delighted customers.

- Every single employee goes through initial training and, at the end of it, they are offered $2,000 to leave. The belief is that those who take the money don't fit the culture anyway (as they're just there for the money).

Social media provides a new avenue when it comes to rewarding behaviour that is in line with your culture and contributes to your positive reputation. Once you are aware of what your employees are saying online, you are in a position to reward them for getting it right. It is possible that you have employees who are incredibly vocal brand ambassadors on social media but you aren't aware of it.

Think of the last time you took an employee aside and told them that there would be an unexpected bonus in the next month's pay packet, or some other reward for a job well done. Have you ever given this type of reward for ambassadorial behaviour or cultural compliance performance? Do managers have the opportunity to say: "Well done for helping to create a great reputation for our business"? Have you given people permission, indeed encouraged people, to talk about the company (within a framework) and do you reward them for doing so?

Consider having a team of official brand ambassadors – people who love the business, are very well-connected online and who can act as amplifiers for all the great stuff you are doing. Sometimes it is just a matter of tapping into the goodwill that already exists, right under your nose. Developing brand ambassadors means helping them to align their short and long-term aspirations with those of the business. And you are better able to reward those ambassadors for the work they already do quite naturally.

It is simply not possible to go into shutdown mode when an employee shares something inappropriate about the business on a social media platform. Seeking to develop a sense of secrecy about how your company operates suggests old-fashioned thinking. Rather, you should focus on ensuring people understand the boundaries and potential impact of what they say, so that they can speak in an appropriate way, but one which is natural to them. By rewarding the people who do this well, you will naturally encourage the behaviour among others on the team.

COPING WITH AN
ALWAYS-ON CULTURE

Employees

A stakeholder has the ability to impact your reputation 24/7. With laptops, tablets and smartphones, your own employees are never more than a click away from their own social media channels or those of the business. This means their actions any time, anywhere – even when away from the workplace – can affect the business's reputation.

Incidentally, although in this section I'm talking about tapping into the 24/7 culture in a positive way, there are some reasons for discouraging such behaviour as well. Harvard Business School professor Leslie Perlow warns us that, "the 'always-on' work culture creates numerous problems for organisations all stemming from the fact that it denies workers a sense of individual efficacy and autonomy by putting them on a permanent state of reactive alert. It drains morale and initiative, and scatters employees' mental resources, making it difficult for them to take ownership of projects and prioritize their efforts."

I agree with the professor's caveat that 24/7 has the potential to give us problems, but for a different reason. Gone are the old-fashioned 9-to-5 workdays more familiar to our grandparents. In recent research carried out by Vodafone and YouGov in the UK, researchers found that more than 60% of business leaders believed that their employees were happier and more productive when they were working in a flexible way.

We know that how people behave – both inside and outside the office – will contribute to your reputation and an increasingly disparate and far-flung workforce makes it even harder to command and control what is being communicated and when. So you need to stop trying. Just get the culture right and your employees' out of office behaviour will look after itself.

As people communicate 24 hours a day on social platforms this is yet another reason for social media monitoring to be considered a must-have. People do make mistakes and you want to rest assured that you have a monitoring system in place that will alert you to anything inappropriate that might have been said (within the bounds of privacy settings, of course). This isn't about dictating what is said or controlling it, but about reacting if a mistake is made.

When an employee makes an honest blunder on social media, how your company deals with it says just as much about your values as what the company itself says, internally and externally. Deal with it within your cultural guidelines. Be loyal to your employee while at the same time demonstrating how seriously you take the situation that has arisen.

According to Simon Clark, Managing Partner at Fidelity Growth Partners Europe, in most cases people will revert to type under pressure. So seeing a person or company under pressure will often reveal the true values of that person or organisation. It's true of entrepreneurs running businesses and it is true of businesses handling crises. So it is important to have a plan in place for how you deal with issues in the public domain, under pressure.

Social media is the great megaphone

"An organisation's reputation is not built on what it claims to be but rather on what its key stakeholders say it is. Social media not only gives our customers, clients and other stakeholders a voice, it amplifies them and makes them accessible on a global scale and at unprecedented speed. What is said about you in London can affect how you're perceived in Johannesburg and vice versa very quickly."

Antony Jenkins, CEO, Barclays Bank

Needless to say, it's not just employee activity that you should be aware of. Perhaps more important is customer activity, both positive and negative. Even major global brands can get this wrong.

In 2013, I watched in disbelief as a disgruntled passenger took to Twitter to vent his anger at the way British Airways was handling the issue of his father's lost luggage. Businessman Hasan Syed decided to pay to have his tweet promoted, targeting US and UK markets to make sure his message reached a wide audience of BA customers (and presumably BA itself). The tweet read: "Don't fly @BritishAirways. Their customer service is horrendous."

He then followed this up with a series of messages criticising BA's delayed response and pledging to continue running Twitter ads (promoted tweets) until the company resolved the problem. Within six hours of the promoted tweet going live, it was picked up and retweeted by the widely-read news site Mashable and the VP of Marketing at JetBlue Airways, among others.

However, it took a further four hours (*after* the Mashable story had run) for BA to pick up on the issue with the response: "Sorry for the delay in responding, our Twitter feed is open 09:00 – 17:00 GMT. Please DM (direct message) your baggage ref and we'll look into this."

The story was covered in the *Guardian*, *Daily Mail*, *Daily Telegraph*, NBC, Fox News and the BBC, among others. The Mashable story has to date been shared more than 20,000 times on social media sites. Syed says he spent at least $1,000 on the promoted tweet, but what was the financial impact of the damage done to BA's reputation?

BA later publicly apologised for the inconvenience caused to Mr Syed with the statement: "We would like to apologise to the customer for the inconvenience caused. We have been in contact with the customer, and the bag is due to be delivered today."

This story is interesting for two reasons. The first is the obvious lack of round-the-clock monitoring which is so critical in today's world. Second, and equally important, is the tone of the initial response via Twitter. Referring to the Twitter feed's opening hours smacks of old-fashioned thinking and a lack of operational understanding of the impact that social channels can have on reputation. Would the cost of having the Twitter feed monitored and manned 24/7 outweigh the potential damage that all this negative coverage created?

THE DANGER OF A CULTURAL VACUUM

I'll finish this chapter on culture by looking at an example where the lack of culture led to gross error and catastrophic loss of reputation.

On 6 July 2013 a train carrying oil to a Canadian refinery derailed and exploded, leaving at least 24 confirmed dead and a further 26 missing. The Montreal Maine & Atlantic Railway was roundly criticised for its communications in the wake of the tragedy. As an outsider it was clear to me that:

- The company had no plan in place to ensure top management arrived at the scene quickly.

- The company delayed in empathising with those affected (from an outsider's perspective, it appeared it was frightened of inadvertently admitting liability).

- It failed to take any form of ownership of the tragedy.

- The fact that the primary spokesperson put forward by the company did not speak French, in a French-speaking province, rubbed salt into the wound.

As it does in disaster situations, the Twittersphere went crazy, with the vast majority of people expressing not only sadness but outrage at the company. At the time of writing, months after the tragedy, there are hourly tweets using the #LacMegantic tag, extending the effect of the story well beyond a traditional news cycle. Maine & Atlantic has since gone out of business. The bankruptcy proceedings are running parallel to several wrongful death and injury lawsuits filed after the crash.

ASK YOURSELF...

- Is the real culture of our business aligned with the desired culture?

- Do I believe our culture supports a positive reputation?

- How could I empower others to reinforce culturally positive behaviour?

- Do our systems and processes support (or detract from) our company culture?

- Can all our employees name the company's core values (unprompted)? Why not ask them?

CHAPTER 6

Are You Being Experienced?

IT'S MORE THAN
JUST BEING HEARD

Are your important stakeholders experiencing the feelings that you would expect when they interact with your company? Are they impressed? Happy? Frustrated? Is every single member of your team living and breathing your core values, and working towards a common goal? It's about every person in the company understanding that it is actions, not words, that reinforce the key messages and perceptions you want to communicate to the outside world. It is one thing to have stated core values, but quite another to know with confidence that your employees' activities are in line with them day in, day out.

You can also check what message the outside world is experiencing by looking inwards. How your people communicate among themselves has always been important, but social media makes it even more so.

I am constantly surprised by the negative comments I see even in my own social networking sphere. People talk disparagingly and very openly about the companies they work for. If your own employees can't be ambassadors for your brand, how can you expect customers to be? The path to a strong reputation truly starts at home. That, in turn, emerges from how you treat your employees. In my experience, happy people mean happy customers. What you see and hear internally is a good guide to what people are experiencing from the outside.

TURNING CORE VALUES INTO
WIDESPREAD BEHAVIOUR

The past few years have seen a lot of business experts dissing old-school command and control models for a more collaborative approach to leadership and management. In terms of the reputation economy this makes sense. After all, you don't have control of your reputation; you only have influence. You need to collaborate with your stakeholders, whoever they may be.

There are no greater potential allies in the quest to influence employee behaviour than the people in the internal communications team. In looking at the purpose, core values and the related, desired behaviours, the internal communications experts are perfectly positioned to create an environment to make it happen, rather than simply telling people what the values are. This is a key strategic role.

In their book *The Social Organisation*, Anthony J. Bradley and Mark P. McDonald say:

"Being a social organisation goes beyond experimenting with social media tools – the provide and pray approach. In fact it's not about the technology at all. A social organisation addresses significant business challenges and opportunities using the social media platform to create mass collaboration."

If you are doing this properly, that is ensuring that widespread behaviour supports core values, and if you buy into the concept of a *social organisation*, you will have to make organisational and structural changes to the way you do business. This is simply because the platforms and technology for working in a social way did not exist ten years ago.

Barclays: committing to a global set of values

When banking regulators on both sides of the Atlantic fined Barclays around £300m for taking part in a series of fraudulent actions aimed at manipulating Libor (the interest rate on which European and North American banks and others base their interest rates), the company's reputation was called into question at the most fundamental level.

Amid widespread media coverage, the then chairman and CEO, Bob Diamond, resigned. Barclays had to initiate efforts to rebuild trust with the public and investors. Recognising that what was required was widespread behaviour change, the solution needed to:

- Solicit the genuine views and perceptions of employees.

- Communicate the values established by new leadership across Barclays.

- Make sure that any online conversation was fairly structured as people at Barclays weren't very aware of social media.

- Show from the outset that things were really going to change.

- Galvanise the bank around its purpose, values and behaviours.

The starting point was an open letter from Antony Jenkins, the new CEO, which made it crystal clear that everyone who did not share Barclays' values had to go. Simple as that. The media gave this wide publicity.

The bank held a series of internal values workshops. This was a big move to get the staff on board with the company's values. It also left the staff in no possible doubt that things were changing and it motivated them to welcome those changes.

So how did Barclays use social media? It played a key role in supporting collaboration and engaging a globally dispersed audience. The company set up a 'values jam' – an online conversation lasting three days, running 24 hours a day. For this, it partnered with IBM both to create the platform and to help evaluate the success and results afterwards. Staff all over the world were engaged with the jam which meant that senior management also had an opportunity to understand them better.

Day 1 was interesting. Conversation was very positive. It was, in fact, so positive that it plainly couldn't be the full view across Barclays. So they got senior people into the conversation to say, "You're being too positive, tell us what's really on your mind." This was the most important part of the values project, with 50% of the 140,000 staff registering to participate. For many, this was the first time they had ever been asked for, or expressed, their views.

The top 150 executives in Barclays got involved to steer the conversation. They would come into the communications centre in London. For much of their business lives they are pre-briefed for meetings and conversations but for this interaction there was no briefing, which made it very interesting. The organisers had to encourage the executives to go for it with their conversations but once they got going they were really into it.

Social media made a huge contribution to the change project that Barclays went through, and continues to go through today. Lots of Barclays people had said that social media wasn't relevant to their part of the business, because of legal or compliance issues, and suddenly it was quite clear that they were wrong. Having these big interventions created a cultural pulse across the organisation. Staff relished having their voices heard in a forum, sharing opinions and having an impact on how the values were rolled out and how management would engage people in the future.

Barclays is planning more jams in the future, on more specific topics. Getting people to interact with each other and show how they feel about working in the company has paid dividends.

MIND ANY GAP BETWEEN
BEHAVIOUR AND CORE VALUES:
THAT'S WHERE THE RISKS ARE

We've talked a lot about purpose and core values being an important starting point when it comes to business reputation. This is where we need to look at strong reputation versus good reputation – because having a strong reputation builds your business. If your behaviour is in line with your core values, customers and employees get what they expect. It's when gaps in the two occur that trouble arises.

Ryanair is a good example of a company with a strong reputation; but a reputation for, in the end, being pretty awful to people. At the time of writing, although Ryanair is anticipating a fall in profits, passenger and revenue growth have continued. Interestingly, the head of Ryanair, Michael O'Leary, has recently been reported to be initiating change. His simple business model has traditionally been "we pick you up and land you on time and that's it." But it would appear that's not enough. He now thinks he needs to augment the service and burnish the company's reputation by being nicer to people. He has put up with years of mainstream media, tweets and emails lashing out at his company, but it was allegedly a face-to-face encounter with an angry customer that backed up all the electronic abuse, and was the final straw in his decision to make changes. This, and a frank admission from his company that its reputation had allowed its rival easyJet to beat it hollow in attracting the business traveller market.

Michael O'Leary achieved the widespread implementation of his core values but is having to review those values in the light of events. One might question whether the people in the business who've supported the *get them there on time and cheaply* behaviour are the same people who will now be able to be more customer-service focused. I have my doubts.

Starbucks provides an example of misalignment of core values and behaviour. People used both traditional and social media to criticise the company over the handling of its tax affairs. Whether they made the connection or not, I believe the public sensed the company's behaviour was in direct contrast to its core values. The coffee chain's stated mission is to be a good neighbour and to contribute to communities where it operates. There was clearly a conflict between what Starbucks said was important and the company's behaviour, and people took action. They stopped going to its coffee shops.

In the UK, Starbucks made a voluntary payment of £20 million payable over a period of time following a very public outcry over its actions. But people saw through it.

Would all this have been avoided if the finance executives understood the impact that their actions could have on the brand's reputation? Did the Chief Risk Officer have a reputation-focused sparring partner, as we discussed in Section One?

In any given issue that spreads widely in mainstream and national media I've found that if you go back and look at the company's purpose and core values, you will find a disconnect with how that company has behaved and that's often what sparked the issue.

A fairly recent example is with telecoms providers in Canada. As at 2013, American mobile providers could not offer competitive services in Canada – but this was all about to change, with discussions around the potential introduction of the US provider Verizon. The venom that the average Canadian spouts about the incumbents, Rogers, Telus and Bell says it all. They are seen as dramatically over-priced and offering very little value compared to their American neighbours. A quick look at their websites suggests core values like "delivering great value and choice" (Rogers), "embrace change and initiate opportunity" (Telus) and "ethical behaviour" (Bell), are completely at odds with how these companies were behaving. It is no wonder that the prospect of a new market entrant created a media storm, online and offline. There are always two sides to a story, of course, but when I spent two weeks in Canada while this story was in the news, the issue was very much part of the mainstream dialogue with very little positive commentary on all three Canadian brands.

The three big companies poured oil on the fire by running an ad campaign complaining that the Canadian government was being biased towards foreign competitors.

Suppose that the companies, instead of boasting that they were already delivering great value, had tried an approach more congruent with their values: "We are striving to improve our service and value for money." Just a thought. They took their eye off the ball and did not concern themselves with what customers were actually experiencing.

SOCIAL MEDIA: THE GREAT AMPLIFIER

If you participate in any social media platforms personally, one campaign that will have been hard to miss is personal care brand Dove's ongoing Campaign for Real Beauty. Ad agency Ogilvy & Mather produced a short video inspired by research findings that suggested only 4% of women describe themselves as beautiful. The firm hired a criminal sketch artist to draw several women (whom he could not see) based on how they described themselves, as well as sketches based on how a stranger described them. When the sketches were compared, the ones created based on strangers' opinions were shown to be invariably more flattering and accurate.

The video has been viewed more than 56 million times. Only with social media could a company get that breadth of audience for such material. The ad sparked discussion and debate, even more closely aligning the Dove brand with a drive for positive body image among all women. This was a good example of great content supporting a company's values and enhancing its reputation.

Consider whether or not you are using social media as a platform to get your story out there and to help people *experience* your brand. As the CEO, are you genuinely walking the talk? Of course, being present on social media won't suit everyone, but I think you need to disregard the power of it only when you have really thought about it. Social platforms help you get your story heard, in the way you believe it should be told. It's the most powerful way to connect directly with those audiences you identified in an earlier chapter. It puts some of the reputation-shaping power back into your own hands.

ASK YOUR TEAM...

- What more could we be doing to build trust in our people and our business, in the first place with customers and employees?

- Are we setting a positive example for our staff, not only in terms of communication, but also in best practice when using social media?

- Do we really understand the value and opportunity that social media could afford our business? Or do we focus primarily on the threat?

CHAPTER 7

Youth Does Not Equal Knowledge

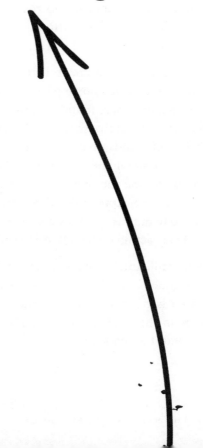

In 2010 and again in 2012, global PR agency Edelman conducted a fascinating study into *millennials* (those born between 1980 and 1995) and how they engage with brands. The research, involving 4,000 millennials in 11 countries, offered very useful insights for businesses wanting to tap into millennials' buying power in the marketplace, but it also shone a light on the mindset of millennials in the workplace. With millennials as the biggest incoming wave of talent, understanding them is critical to appreciating how they can help hard-wire core values into your business's DNA.

In the marketplace, millennials are connected more by their communal use of the global network than by ethnicity, economic or social class, age or gender. This means that it's becoming more important to reach out to a group of people who are linked by something like Facebook than it is to consider what will appeal to a particular age or gender group.

According to the research, a millennial's key consideration when making a buying decision is peer reviews and recommendations. The Edelman report found that millennials see themselves as potential brand ambassadors and that eight-in-ten take action on behalf of brands (that is, they promote them to other people they believe should be interested). They're loyal. Seven-in-ten keep purchasing the brands they love and they see brands as a form of self-expression. They may be susceptible to and addicted to brands, but they also want to see all the facts before they'll take action on behalf of a brand – so transparency is key.

By 2025 millennials will account for 70% of the global workforce, so the time to pay attention to them is now. Assuming this research is right, we have to take it very seriously; it's a big change in the market and demands an equally big change in the mindset of marketers.

What does this mean for your business, your reputation strategy and your treatment of social media? A few things spring to mind and you need to look at this from two angles – when millennials are buying from you and when they're joining and working for your organisation.

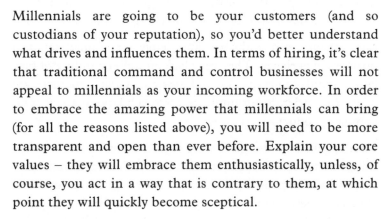

Use millennials for their strengths

Make good use of the millennials in your company. Encourage divisions and departments to hire them for their social media knowledge and their genuinely passionate approach to more transparent and meaningful business.

Millennials are going to be your customers (and so custodians of your reputation), so you'd better understand what drives and influences them. In terms of hiring, it's clear that traditional command and control businesses will not appeal to millennials as your incoming workforce. In order to embrace the amazing power that millennials can bring (for all the reasons listed above), you will need to be more transparent and open than ever before. Explain your core values – they will embrace them enthusiastically, unless, of course, you act in a way that is contrary to them, at which point they will quickly become sceptical.

Purpose and core values matter to these people. If they believe in your business and work for your business, you can be sure that their whole focus will be on living the core values. They probably won't hesitate to call you or others to account on it when you are not living your core values yourself.

What you should not do is hire a millennial simply to run your business' social media. In most businesses I interact with, whether they are agencies, start-ups or large corporates, this tends to be the case: the day-to-day handling of social media is often left to the youngest person on the team. Often they are millennials. Particularly at the lower end of the millennial age range, they *get* social media, they're young, social media is a *kid's thing* and we can leave it to them, right? Well, maybe not.

IS AN INTERN RESPONSIBLE FOR YOUR REPUTATION?

Having said all that about the power of millennials, it's important to remember the value of experience in planning and running a business. The enthusiasm, energy, fresh-thinking and values-driven passion of millennials will take them far but probably, unless they're geniuses and they make their own rules, not as far as taking charge. At least, not yet.

Back them with industry knowledge and financial and business experience. They may lack an understanding of how large organisations operate and how particular structures are needed in order, for example, to approach large markets with complex products.

I am appalled by the number of organisations I meet who are using interns, often unpaid, to act as the eyes, ears and sometimes voice of the organisation. They put them in charge of social media and beyond that make them responsible for deciding what is brought to management's attention. It's potentially dangerous for the business, but it is also unfair on the millennial. The real opportunity here lies in bringing together the energy and passions of youth with the insights and sure-footedness of experience.

First, there is nothing wrong with the youngest person, or people, on your team running the day-to-day social media feeds, with the right infrastructure to support them. In fact, because they have grown up in this all-communicating, hyper-connected world, it often makes good sense. But, it is important that you do two things:

1. Train the people acting as your face to the outside world to within an inch of their lives. Teach them about your business, your products and services, and about your core values and what these mean in terms of how the business operates and communicates. This is the relatively easy bit and you've probably already done it – but have you tested it? Regularly throw some really tough questions at them and ask how they'd respond if that was posed publicly. Role play a couple of devastating tweets and see how they react. Remember that people revert to type under pressure. These people are probably in your PR or marketing departments but the business training will likely take them into other parts of the business and even on to training courses in different functions. The person you're training is going to become a truly cross-functional front of house.

2. Give them absolute, genuine authority to act in line with your core values. That will mean spending money to make someone's day. A Zappos call centre operator sent flowers to a customer whose husband had died. A famous steakhouse delivered steak to a regular customer, who also happens to be a prolific Twitter user, upon landing at Newark airport. For how not to do this, look at how an airline recently handled the case of a man who was flying home early because his wife and two children had been killed in a tragic fire. The airline chose to charge the man for a full ticket since he was changing the date of his flight. The story was shared far and wide, and, without knowing the detail, I would be willing to bet that the reputational damage far outweighed the potential cost of flying him home on a different flight at no extra cost. Examples like these are endless. Do you want an inexperienced team member making these decisions?

- Who is in charge of our social media feeds? How are they being empowered and supported?

- Are we monitoring the use of our brand in social media, even if we are not present in social channels currently?

- What are we doing to attract top millennial talent?

CHAPTER 8

Behaviour (Not PR) Drives Reputation

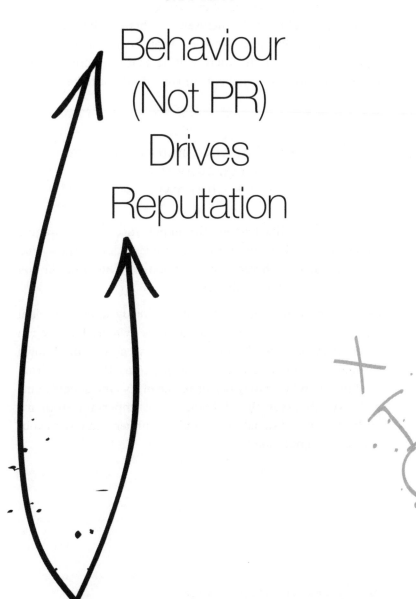

ARE YOU A SOCIAL ORGANISATION?

A social organisation lives by collaboration. In business terms this extends well beyond social media and involves all your stakeholders in defining and reinforcing your reputation. It can also become a source of enduring competitive advantage as each stakeholder tucks themselves in behind the company's purpose. We have seen Google, Apple, Amazon and many others achieve this; and there will be others specific to your sector, no matter how niche. Can you afford not to be there?

REINFORCING BEHAVIOUR THAT SUPPORTS YOUR CORE VALUES

We've already talked about the importance of encouraging company-wide behaviour that reinforces your purpose and core values, and thereby your reputation. But how do you hard-wire it into your culture?

In my experience, the best leaders already know the right questions to ask about the organisation as a whole. This section is about identifying the questions to ask as you drill down through the organisation. These questions lean away from the figures and everyday performance of specific departments and towards areas that I know to be important from my understanding of social media and the influence it has on your company's reputation.

Let's start with the most common functions in large organisations. If we don't cover an area that is critical for your business, you'll quickly see a pattern emerging in the types of questions you need to ask and you should be able to tweak what's here accordingly. We'll take it function by function.

CUSTOMER SERVICE

There was a time when the only ways a customer could communicate with a business were by letter or telephone. Then came the boom in call centres, which evolved from simple voice (remember those endless menus?) to email and then instant messenger chat. Today, social platforms like Facebook and Twitter are very quickly emerging as the first port of call for customers who have questions, complaints or compliments. And review sites like TripAdvisor, Amazon and even Google+ give customers access to the wisdom of crowds as they consider making a purchase.

Acknowledging this fundamental shift in how people communicate requires a shift in thinking about how you do things within the customer service department. You need to train your customer service people differently if they are going to be communicating frequently, every day and on a public stage. They need to understand the fragile nature of reputation, even one that starts off strong (think of the companies who outsourced their call centres to people whose English was not up to the job – the frustration customers felt did more harm than good). Your customer service training should get your teams to nurture your reputation any way they can and should be completely in line with how you want the brand to be perceived. Simply knowing the mechanics of how to tweet, post and generate audience engagement is good, but the trick is to check that they truly contribute to your brand's positive reputation.

According to a 2012 study of 2000 people in the USA by Edison Research – called 'The Social Habit' – 32% of respondents who had attempted to contact a brand or company through social media for customer support expected a response within 30 minutes. A further 42% expected a response within 60 minutes. Is your company prepared to handle social media inquiries within the hour? Do you even know these questions are being asked?

Another recent study by Conversocial looked specifically at Twitter for customer service. After reviewing more than 40,000 tweets to gauge how well American brands were really using Twitter as a customer service channel, the resulting report found 42% of brands who initially responded to customers completely ignored subsequent customer tweets when the customer declined to move the discussion to phone or email.

Not surprisingly, 19% of customers said they had already tried the suggested alternative channel, or they preferred communicating via Twitter. Imagine that – completely ignoring an unhappy customer, who has aired a complaint publicly. Some interesting headline findings from the report include:

- Verizon, JC Penney, Bank of America and American Airlines all deflected less than 3% of tweets to traditional customer service channels (Verizon was the best, deflecting just 0.21%).

- Lowes, Delta, T-Mobile and Wells Fargo deflected the most tweets in their industries, with Lowes sending more than 23% of customer inquiry tweets away from social media and back to traditional channels.

- Airlines and telecoms companies deflected the fewest tweets on average (2%), while restaurants deflected the most on average (21%).

This creates a challenge for brands, particularly consumer brands who want to be able to engage with customers in the way that they choose, but don't want to create a public platform for airing dirty laundry. You will need to think carefully about how to handle the eventuality of heavy, nasty criticism, whether it's justified or not. If you are likely to encounter that issue, consider having an @[brand name]help Twitter handle and Facebook page for now. That creates a focus area to prioritise customer service issues and leaves the general brand page free for other communications and conversation.

For B2B businesses, it's worth reflecting on whether you know how your customers want to interact with you. I was in a meeting recently where a senior partner at an accounting firm was asked if he had an app for his customers. He didn't. The person asking then pulled out his iPhone to demonstrate what his accountant's app did. It was an app with several functions that his customers found very useful – a quick cash-flow report, a break-even calculator and a simple return on investment estimator, for example.

Now is the time to challenge your own thinking about how you serve your customers. If you don't, you may be missing an opportunity as your competition steams ahead. The people you want to reach will almost inevitably be talking online about your company, your competition and issues affecting your industry. How is your company dealing with it?

Sample questions to ask your customer service/experience team include:

- Do we know what our customers are saying about us on social media?

- Do we track people who are openly dissatisfied with our competitors? And then pass the insight on to the sales team?

- Where are the skeletons in our closet when it comes to customer service? How would we react if these were discussed openly on social media platforms?

- What are we doing to mitigate that risk?

- What could we do better when it comes to customer service? Can technology make it happen?

- If we have customer service channels on social media, are the best people running those channels? Are they empowered to act?

- How are we currently measuring customer service? Is there a better way?

LEGAL

In many businesses, the legal team is seen as the team that puts a stop to things, the sales *prevention* department. They necessarily err on the side of caution. They're picky about the details of a deal. For our purposes here, this is not about putting in place more rules and regulations. It's about ensuring the entire business knows what the new reputation economy looks like and how they should behave within it in order for the business to thrive.

Legal teams that delay responses or recommend "No comment" are probably aiming to protect the business, but could have a damaging affect on reputation.

Companies must work within the law, of course, but part of taking on a more human face means potentially taking some legal risks. Take the mobile operator O2 network shutdown which prompted customer outrage. An old-fashioned company would have used a 'safe' approach, for example: "We are doing our best to resolve the issue and will keep you updated." I am certain the lawyers would have slept well at night knowing that that's what was being said. But to customers coping without their critical mobile service, it would have been like a red rag to a bull! What they need to hear is "I'm sorry."

Walking a fine line: the O2 story

UK mobile operator O2 had a major network failure. Customers took to social media platforms to vent their fury and frustration. With nearly a quarter of a million online mentions and close to 200,000 retweets, the business was faced with the potential for major reputational damage. With a careful and skilful response strategy, O2 was not only able to calm the wildfire of malicious customer comments, but also garnered the respect of the thousands of Twitter users (many of whom were customers) looking on.

The clever part of the strategy was not to hide behind the classic "Sorry, but things are beyond our control … we regret this inconvenience and will get back to normal as fast as possible." Rather, company representatives responded like a pal, answering every tweet separately, making the delivery of information more impactful by answering each customer in a very personal manner. It was also careful not to diminish the inconvenience that it was clearly causing.

This came from the O2 Twitter feed:

Customer (@24vend_Ltd): "@O2 had to travel to Italy to get signal – desperate times!!!"

O2 response: "You can come back now. We're back in business :)"

I think the important message is to ensure your legal counsel is up to date with what they need to do to protect the company in the social media age. So, the questions are:

- What are the guidelines when it comes to social media and the law – have any recent precedents been set and what can we learn from them?

- Are we prepared to express and distribute in simple, layman's terms what these guidelines are?

- Should we be reconsidering our own policies and procedures when it comes to crisis planning?

- (Particularly in heavily regulated industries) is there a governing body that has an opinion on how businesses use social media?

- Do you personally engage in social media? Are you on LinkedIn? Do you participate in relevant legal discussions?

- Are we sure that all our IP and trademarks are protected on current social media platforms? Do we own our Twitter handle, Facebook page name, YouTube channel? (Even if you do little or nothing with them, at least if you have them you can control what goes on them.)

- And in an age of *hacktivism* do we own all potentially negative domains – [yourcompany]sucks.com for example?

OPERATIONS

This is where things start to get very interesting. If core values are how things *are* done around here then the operations function might be how things *get* done around here. I believe operations has the biggest potential to make an impact on your reputation. Let's go back to *The Social Organisation*, by Anthony Bradley and Mark McDonald. I don't think this book got the recognition it deserved. What it highlighted was the fundamental need for a shift in corporate culture (both internally and externally) from being centrally directed to being focused on collaboration. Are you willing to ask the really tough questions and consider the potential to undertake some major organisational change? Well, nobody said life was easy. Here's a starting point:

- Do our systems and processes create a desire for our employees to be engaged? Or are they seen as needless bureaucracy? If the latter, have we asked them how they'd prefer things to be done?

- How could we benefit from better collaboration within the various business functions?

- Are there obvious opportunities for collaboration that would benefit our customers?

- Are competing factions within the business stopping us from being as successful as we might otherwise be? Time and again I witness turf wars between marketing and PR departments. I have heard stories of different banking channels cannibalising their own business just to meet KPIs (for example, call centres creating new applications from those that were started online, in order to get the tick in the box).

- Do we regularly get data and insights from our social media monitoring reports? If not, why not? If so, how can we better use the data?

IT

The importance of the IT department has shot up over the past 25 years. What was once a group of smart, introverted whiz kids has grown into a department that understands, supports and is usually critical to the strategic imperatives of the business.

Whether it is ensuring that all employees remain connected (these days people break into a sweat if their email is down for more than a minute), or focusing on the future roadmap of the business, there is no denying that in a business of any size, the IT department is critical.

So, if this is true, shouldn't it be right at the heart of any discussion about reputation? Time and again I see people tweeting complaints about their systems being down. There's even a hashtag (a pointer to an open conversation on a topic) on Twitter called #IThell.

My suspicion is that often the IT issues people complain about are related to user error. But whatever the cause, any glitch that is talked about publicly gives a bad impression of your business both internally and externally.

Of course genuine, large-scale technology issues can have a direct impact on your customers and on your reputation. Just look at this example from NatWest:

NatWest: computer says no

In the UK, a major computer failure caused disruption for RBS, NatWest and Ulster Bank customers for several days in 2012 and again in 2013. Some businesses were unable to pay clients, shoppers were short of cash because bank machines refused to pay out, and some were even left stranded at the check-out. Home movers suffered extra stress, worried that delayed transactions might put back the handover of keys.

The bank brought thousands of people in at weekends to tackle the problem – the cost of paying additional staff overtime alone is understood to have run into millions of pounds. And that's before the company started to pay compensation to millions of customers. According to the *Daily Telegraph*:

"Investec Securities banks analyst Ian Gordon said that while the problems were the 'worst mass outage in living memory' he expected the final bill to the bank to come in at between £50m and £100m".

Here is an offline problem that was amplified by social media, adding untold additional costs to the already enormous numbers.

So when you get to the IT people here are the questions to ask:

- How do we build the culture of the company into systems design?
- Is your team aware of its contribution towards the reputation of the business?
- How are we preparing for the greatest potential risks to our business when it comes to technology failure?
- Are there triggers in place for your team to alert the communications team at the first sign of an issue that might affect customer service (but *before* we get customer calls)?
- Does your team monitor social media to spot potential technology issues before they escalate?
- Do you have access to social media monitoring data that is already collated by the marketing/PR/customer service teams? If not, would it be useful?
- Do we use technology tools to collaborate effectively internally? Or could we be doing better in this area?

SALES, MARKETING, COMMUNICATIONS

As the outward-facing people in your business, I would expect that this group is the most switched on when it comes to social media and reputation.

Although traditional marketing and PR principles still apply in today's world, subtle shifts are taking place that cannot be ignored. As a useful summary of these changes, advertising giant Ogilvy has updated the traditional four Ps of marketing (product, price, place, promotion) to become the four Es:

Product to **Experience**: Instead of thinking about the qualities of the product, focus on what a customer experiences when using your product or service. Or even broader, what is the entire brand experience (from entering shops to calling customer support)?

Price to **Exchange**: No longer simply about lowest price, these days the market looks far more at value. What are you willing to offer your customers in exchange for their attention, custom and loyalty?

Place to **Everyplace**: Today, the brands that surround us are the brands that win. Be in the right place, at the right time, wherever that may be. And interact with a customer in a way that feels natural and seamless, rather than an unwanted interruption.

Promotion to **Evangelism**: We live in an all-communicating world. And it is a world where people want to see a company's passion in its communications. When the focus becomes creating a product or service so powerful that it generates its own independent evangelists (by way of customers) you've hit the jackpot.

This is where we start to pull together the theory we have talked about up until now and ask critical questions of the team around you:

- Are our latest marketing campaigns connected to a single core driver that is so ingrained it does not shift each time there's a new marketing director?

- How are we using social media to show, not tell, whatever we are trying to communicate? Give me examples.

- What could I be doing on social media to support your efforts?

- What's our plan for social media, should disaster strike? (Even if we have a stated strategy to remain off social media platforms.)

- Do we have 24-hour social media monitoring in place? Who gets notified of an issue and how?

FINANCE

Today, people in the finance department need to have a strong understanding of reputation and the roles they play within it. Taking risks with the company's money is one thing; taking risks with its reputation is another. The financial services industry has major reputation-related issues (which was one of the reasons I was so interested to get the views of Barclays' Antony Jenkins for this book). We've talked a lot about ensuring behaviour is aligned with values. I believe businesses should pay special attention to this when it comes to money.

That brings us to questions to ask our finance team:

- As a company, do our financial practices align with our core values? For example, if our goal is to be a friend to small business on the sales side, do we pay our own small suppliers promptly?

- What systems do we have in place to monitor finance-related discussions about our company on social media? Do we have a nominated individual who responds?

- When we have upcoming financial news, do we make good use of the impacts that social channels have across our priority financial markets?

- Are we monitoring what activist investors and commentators are saying about us, our competition and our industry (remember Icahn's single tweet about Apple that I mentioned earlier).

- Are finance-related social media reports being shared as a result of our social media monitoring/analytics?

IT'S CONTROL,
BUT NOT AS WE KNEW IT

Control is not a dirty word. When it comes to social channels, there is nothing wrong with wanting to take control. And you can. But the control lies somewhere other than you might think. It is no longer about the ability to drip-feed information to the market or employees, old-school broadcast style. In the reputation economy, control comes from real-time knowledge, from monitoring social channels and using predefined criteria (positive and negative) to trigger a reaction from your business.

You cannot control negative things people will say about you, but you can do two things: manage how you react (negatives create the most wonderful opportunities for great reputation-building) and manage how you reward and encourage positive sentiment towards the business. Equally, you can control how much the people in your company understand about the impact of their actions, online and off, on your company's reputation. Preparation and knowledge will undoubtedly give you the edge.

Keeping track of success

Do you have a plan to challenge every department's awareness of its contribution to company reputation?

ASK YOUR BOARD...

- In which area of our business do you see the greatest exposure to reputational risk?

- Is there more we could be doing to address the issue of reputation?

- Do we routinely address reputation with business functions other than customer service and marketing?

SECTION THREE

Building a
Reputation
Strategy

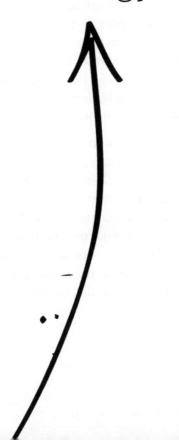

We've looked at the rise of corporate reputation and the implications of social media. We've also explored how to build a company's purpose and core values into your culture, with a focus on behaviour.

This section starts to get a lot more practical. I will address ways to exploit and improve your reputation by taking a good look at who you are and how you can use your personality and tone of voice – as a company – to contribute to your desired reputation. We'll look at the opportunities created by building and engaging with communities, by creating compelling content and we'll also start to identify how you might use social media (and if it is worth looking at, based on your target audiences). I've also included a chapter on handling a crisis – when it comes to social media, the potential for a crisis to start or spread online is the single biggest issue keeping many of the CEOs I speak to awake at night.

This section also provides insight into the practicalities of creating a reputation strategy and making it work. As with any good strategy, reputation management needs careful planning. It is critical to understand where you are as a business and to get alignment on where you want to be. I highly recommend that you spend time thinking about the questions I raise in Chapter 9 and discussing them with your senior team. Ultimately the plan is going to be as good as the thinking that goes into it, so don't shortchange yourself at this vital first step.

CHAPTER 9

Putting a Reputation Strategy in Place

WHAT IS A REPUTATION
STRATEGY?

As CEO you have a vision for your business, underpinned by a particular ethos, and a message you want to convey. Communicating that vision to your most senior team with passion, energy and enthusiasm is easy when you do it in person – it's not difficult to get the people you work with directly to buy in. However, getting that vision and the company's desired reputation woven into the fabric of the organisation at every level is more difficult and requires a well thought-through strategy. Starting with the cultural focus we outlined in the previous section is critical.

A reputation strategy is simply the articulation of what you want to be known for and how you intend to get there. It pulls all the elements we've already addressed together and adds communications to the mix.

A reputation strategy must be authentic to your brand, well documented and well communicated. Similar to any other strategy, it will include an analysis of how things stand today, and objectives and tasks for the future. Building a strong reputation takes time and requires that everyone in the organisation pulls together in exactly the same direction – your strategy will set out how this is going to be done.

WHY DOES REPUTATION
STRATEGY MATTER?

Without a reputation strategy the risk of catastrophic damage is high and the potential for profitably leveraging your reputation is low. Think back to the Maine & Atlantic case study we addressed earlier, where an effective strategy was apparently absent. Particularly in today's media landscape, reputation is the currency that drives a business's success or contributes to its demise. The business strategy dictates what people are going to achieve, the reputation strategy reinforces how they are going to act. It clearly defines what behaviour you expect from those in your organisation and from the organisation as a whole.

DIRECT THE BEHAVIOUR OF
YOUR ORGANISATION

The best communications plan is unable to compensate for a poor business plan (you can't spin your way to victory), but a solid business plan can be greatly enhanced by good communications if the two walk hand-in-hand. Social media makes this truer than ever. Your reputation will only survive and thrive if what you're doing is what you're saying – if you're walking the walk, not just talking the talk.

Putting a reputation strategy in place at the centre of the organisation – and requiring everyone to work in accordance with it – is essential. Your business can only act in accordance with its purpose and values if there is a reputation strategy that defines how the business should behave and communicate. When you have this strategy in position it gives your communications team something to work to as they communicate with the outside world and, more importantly, as they steer the culture of the organisation on the inside.

Harold Burson, founder of one of the world's largest PR agencies, Burson-Marsteller, suggests communications teams don't look inwards enough. He talks about the changing nature of PR and points out that there has been too much emphasis on the communications aspect of the discipline rather than on its ability to change behaviour. Over time, the public relations discipline has narrowed, becoming focused almost entirely on *communicating* to the world. The PR department has seemingly willingly accepted the role of the company's soapbox.

In my view, the PR department's real (and far more valuable) role is to influence how people within the organisation consistently behave and by so doing build a company's reputation. But to achieve this we need to know where the leaders are taking the business. It is this comprehensive knowledge that enables leaders inside the company to develop their strategies. They can't write their marketing plans, product plans, IT plans and so on unless they understand the purpose, values and goals of the organisation.

> **It starts with culture**
>
> "Banks need to go much further [than repairing their balance sheets] if public trust in our industry is to be rebuilt. This requires cultural change. For me, this starts with having a common purpose and values that serve as a foundation for everything else that you want to achieve. There can be no choice between doing well financially and behaving responsibly in business."
>
> **Antony Jenkins, CEO of Barclays Bank**

Have you communicated your desired reputation for the business in a succinct way? A business can only communicate the right messages if they are driven from the top. The best PR practitioners communicate with the CEO and look at the company's reputation as a whole. This is not simply how you are communicating and what you are communicating, but *why* you are communicating. Does the company's behaviour support both of these areas?

A case in point was the Archbishop of Canterbury's announcement that he was going into competition with Wonga, the high-profile UK payday loan company, by building up Britain's network of credit unions. He made this announcement amid much fanfare, without realising that through the Church of England's pension fund it *owned* a part of Wonga itself. The Church moved from taking the moral high ground to being accused of hypocrisy in a few short hours, due in large part to its focus on communications rather than behaviour.

Case study – behaviour at the heart of a reputation strategy

Doubletree by Hilton is a chain of hotels that expresses its differentiator by promising to "create a rewarding experience (CARE) for our guests. It starts with a warm chocolate chip cookie to welcome you". Note the behaviour. The company's website, advertising and social media presence promote this philosophy.

What is most powerful is the less overt activity which is completely in line with the strategy, but also appealing and relevant to its customers. For example, the company created a campaign clearly aimed at surprising and delighting existing and potential customers. It is summed up by this tweet:

> "In Seattle today? Tell us what #LittleThings would make your day better and we might surprise you. Ride to Airport? Tix to hydro boat race?"

What Doubletree is doing is clever. It is expanding the concept of a rewarding experience to life beyond its hotel rooms. And in so doing, it can reach (and win over) a much broader audience. For the cost of a taxi ride or tickets to an event, the company will have probably secured a future customer, and also created a brand ambassador for life.

Before the advent of social media, such a campaign would arguably have been impossible (or simply would not have made financial sense due to the cost of communicating it).

DEFINING AN EFFECTIVE
REPUTATION STRATEGY

A good reputation strategy reinforces guiding principles for the business as a whole and should remain consistent, no matter who is running the company. It is about what you stand for and what your behaviours are, and it strives for a complete alignment of both.

The communications strategy is a subset of the reputation strategy and is more flexible. It will shift depending on the best current channels to reach your target audiences. And the social media strategy, a subset of the communications strategy, will be even more fluid. By its very nature, a social strategy must be very much of the moment.

> "Proper reputation planning is no longer a 'nice to have'. Increasingly it is being included in corporate governance codes of conduct and may eventually be anchored in legislation. It's an area businesses need to take seriously. And if they are, then the impact of social media will be included by necessity."
>
> **Aileen Thompson, former communications director at Vodafone and Kellogg's**

A solid reputation strategy starts with a long, honest look at what the company is doing well and not so well, right now. You may need research to establish this. It also involves a deep understanding of reputational risk and stakeholder insight – that is, the potential risks to your reputation that exist across the organisation, internally and externally.

Critically, maintaining a good reputation involves keeping your employees up to date with your desired reputation and how you plan to get there. It is really important that every single person in the organisation understands the role that they have to play. The reputation strategy must be deeply interwoven with the business plan, as we have already discussed. In the next chapter I will suggest a typical structure for a reputation strategy, but the format should ideally align with your own business plan.

Here's a model we can use to give a quick steer on where any reputational issues – and as a result attention – may lie. Using your own gut feel, where does your business reputation lie along the reputation axis? Generally, do people have a positive feeling when they think about your business or your brand? Now think about your product – is it exactly as you would like it to be? Are there known weaknesses that you haven't yet addressed? What is the general sentiment from customers when it comes to your product? Whatever quadrant you fall into will offer you some guidance as to what approach you might want to take in your reputation strategy.

REPUTATION STRATEGY STEERING MODEL

STRONG	**Best kept secret** • Audience analysis • Message development • Storytelling • Cultivate relationships	**Winning!** • Keep going • Creative iterations • Remain true to brand
PRODUCT		
WEAK	**Back to basics** • Product • R&D • Process • Review purpose & values	**On thin ice** • Risk of exposure (reputational risk) • Focus on behaviour (product/service) • Look inside first – it all starts with you • Social media risks
	WEAK REPUTATION STRONG	

We have established that the reputation strategy emanates from, and reflects the purpose and core values of, the business. So the starting point is to restate the business's purpose, core values and desired reputation.

I like to use the GOSPA – goals, objectives, strategy, planning and actions – approach to thinking through and documenting a plan. It's a simple framework for any plan to support your business. Let's walk through how a GOSPA might look when creating a reputation strategy. We'll use a fictitious business-to-business supplier of mobile communications services to illustrate the point. As you read this, think about it in the context of your business.

Goals: These should be very high-level and essentially define your desired reputation. For our company it might be to be known as the mobile communications company that will stop at nothing to help its business customers succeed. Such a statement would not necessarily be made public; it may only be for those working in the business to know.

Examples of strong versus weak desired reputation statements

For a low-cost roadside hotel chain:

- **Good**: We want to be known by road warriors for being there when they need us and offering the best night's sleep.

- **Mediocre**: We want to appeal to business people who travel regularly and need a low-cost hotel at convenient locations.

The reason the first works better than the second is because it is human and appeals to something hard-working business travellers dream about at the end of a long day on the road. The second merely states the features of what it offers (low-cost and convenient), which could be applied to many of its competitors.

Objectives: As a result of the clear understanding of the reputational goal, what are the specific, measurable objectives we can set in order to get us there? In this case, the three objectives might be:

1. To increase the new business pipeline of small to medium-sized businesses by 50% over the next 12 months.

2. To be recognised as the go-to people for anything to do with business communications, measured by at least ten inbound expert/journalist/influencer requests over the next six months.

3. To secure five business case studies for use in the public domain within the next six months.

Strategy: In this part of the plan we demonstrate how we are going to achieve the objectives. To achieve the first example objective, the strategy might include an active social media campaign on both Twitter and LinkedIn, where small business owners are known to be present. The activity will be aimed at helping rather than selling; reinforcing the desired reputation that this business will stop at nothing to help business customers succeed. Perhaps the company will offer access to a Twitter chat with a world-famous businessperson or a competition to win a three-month mentorship with someone who has achieved extraordinary business success. There are many possibilities.

For the second objective, the company might create a content-rich website providing insight, top tips and a rich source of videos to help SME business leaders. And for the third objective, rather than simply requesting that existing customers act as case studies, the company might offer something in return. This might be to cover the cost of a video about the customer's success, to be used by both the customer and the business, or to offer a three-month payment holiday for one key service, or to feature the customer in a national advertising campaign. Whatever it is, it must have genuine value to the company's customer in order to reinforce the desired reputation. Remember, everything the company does must send a message: we will stop at nothing to make your business succeed.

This leads us to the **plans**. Plans are specific elements of the strategy. Limited to the short term, 30 to 60 days, they set out milestones towards the objective that let you know you are on the right track.

Finally we come to **actions**. These are the specific activities that named people within the organisation are going to perform in order to achieve the ultimate reputational goals.

Many of the elements within the reputation plan will also relate to behaviour, but may currently be outside the scope of your communications team. For example, if you want your people to walk the talk of *stopping at nothing to help their customers succeed*, what are they empowered to do? Can they drop everything to visit a customer site? Are they authorised to link up two customers who may have mutually beneficial business connections? Do they have authority to refund money? Expedite a payment? The list goes on. Think about the *actions* your people could take, no matter how big or small, that would be valuable and meaningful to your customers.

For example, in reputation management it is often the little things that count. I heard of a small chain of bicycle stores whose employees had the authority to give away anything priced at under a dollar for free. In real terms it cost the business very little, but in the currency of positive reputation it paid dividends.

DO YOUR
PREPARATION WORK

The GOSPA process for creating a reputation strategy is fairly straightforward, but it is the thinking behind the process that will get you where you want to be. Let's go through it in more detail.

Why are you concerned about reputation? Is it a sudden concern because you believe yours has been tarnished by events? Perhaps you believe you have no reputation at all? Or maybe you don't actually know what your reputation is? Why would it benefit you to have a strong reputation?

Going through a logical planning process will turn lists of issues like these into a relevant action plan for your organisation. And most important, it will ensure your company's core values align with the desired reputation.

The starting point in producing a strategy to manage your reputation is to write down your business goals, reputation goals and core values on a chart like the one below, also stating the person responsible for this area. Are there any obvious inconsistencies? If so, you need to address them in a way that is in line with your stated purpose, values and what you want to be known for. As CEO, you need to own this. If you don't know this information off the top of your head, how can you expect your teams to achieve it?

Business goals: We want to achieve …	Person responsible
Core values: The way things are done around here …	Person responsible
Reputation goals: We want to be known for …	Person responsible
Strategy: How are we going to achieve these particular goals?	Person responsible

WHERE YOU STAND TODAY –
SWOT ANALYSIS

Measuring progress in maintaining and improving your reputation is also important if you are going to know whether or not the plan is working. So you need to know where you stand today. You need an analysis of the reputation-related strengths, weaknesses, opportunities and threats – a good old-fashioned SWOT.

Such a SWOT analysis helps you to identify the areas in which you need to set a goal in your reputation management plan. I've chosen, simply as an illustration, eight issues that have a profound effect on reputation in many companies:

- product/service quality (do you have an objective measure?)
- customer service
- environmental/sustainability issues
- financial performance
- business governance
- independent review by external critics
- employee satisfaction and engagement
- effective communications.

In the first place, it's not a bad idea to take a gut-feel approach to the initial measurement of the overall reputation of your organisation. On a scale of 1 to 10 where would you put your reputation against the criteria you have chosen? Repeat the exercise with the management team, without sharing your own answers. And then with the board. Are there inconsistencies? If not, then give yourself a big pat on the back, because that is rare.

Undoubtedly some areas for concern will emerge. It is worth focusing the formal measurement and activity on these areas first. You will also be creating a benchmark for future progress. It is interesting to present this list in radar chart form; it makes it easy to review as people implement plans for reputational improvement throughout the business. The goal is to have a complete circle at the outer edges of the web. You can include the radar diagram, or spider's web, in each department's reputation plan as a common indicator of progress.

RADAR CHART OF REPUTATION ISSUES

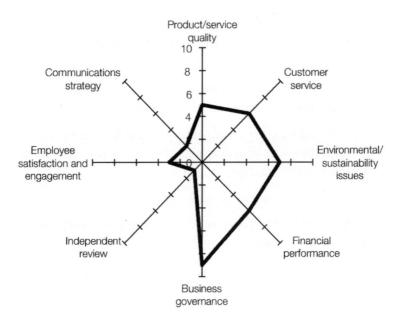

Given the situation in the above diagram, the planning team might select three areas for attention and therefore for goals in the plan – communications strategy, employee engagement and independent review. Remember, as I suggest above, you should focus first on the areas where you have the biggest issue.

Here are possible reputation **goals** in these areas (a single reputational goal for each area):

- *Communications strategy*: to have a communications strategy, including SMART (specific, measurable, achievable, results-focused, time-specific) goals, in place by a specified date.

- *Employee engagement*: to be a sought-after employer.

- *Independent review*: to be the supplier of choice in our niche in our industry, measured by five-star reviews.

Next, write **objectives** against each of these goals (three objectives for each goal):

Communications objectives:

- To form a reputation management steering committee by the end of next month.

- To create the first iteration of a reputation management strategy and plan within the next 60 days.

- To compose and run a company-wide familiarisation course with all employees to disseminate core values and reputation activities within 90 days.

Employee satisfaction objectives:

- To be listed in *The Times* top 100 companies to work for by September next year.

- To carry out a survey to ensure that we understand our own employees' wants and needs.

- To follow up the survey with a plan for action.

Independent review objectives:

- To establish an independent benchmark on our performance by end Q3.

- To use social media to encourage independent review.

- To improve reviews/ratings on public sites (such as TripAdvisor, Amazon and Google+) by 25% within 12 months.

Here it is important to keep thinking about *reputation* as the driver for this plan. What do you want to be known for? Don't get bogged down with communications channels (marketing materials, email campaigns, viral videos, media relations, and the list goes on) just yet – and social media may or may not even be a part of it (unless it is integral to the business area, such as independent review).

Plans are the fun bit. This is where you make sure you are walking the talk. Promulgating and demonstrating your reputation strategy will be part of the plan; nothing will damage your reputation more than if you say one thing and do another.

Finally, think about the **actions** that your team could be taking in the next 30 to 90 days – daily, weekly and monthly – to reach the goals and objectives you outlined at the beginning. What will these actions be? Who will own them?

REPUTATION AT THE HEART
OF THE PLAN

If this is all starting to feel like you are simply reiterating your business plan, go back to step 1 and think about the goals, objectives and strategies specifically in relation to your *reputation*.

And don't worry too much about crossover between business and reputation plans. If there is repetition, it means there is alignment. However, it will be critical to ensure that the implementation phase is well planned to avoid duplication of effort.

It is the CEO's job to put a stake in the ground to determine the company's desired reputation and then build the business to support that. Have you done this? If the outcomes of this process mirror your existing business strategy, the good news is you have the best possible foundations in place – you simply need to weave in the reputational element throughout. Are you focusing on reinforcing behaviour that is in line with your purpose and core values throughout the company? If this is being done it will inevitably reinforce your reputation.

You now have the framework for your reputation strategy.

REPUTATION STEERING
COMMITTEE

Ask most CEOs who owns reputation in their business and many will be hard-pressed to answer. Even for those businesses that do have the equivalent of a Chief Reputation Officer, for the most part these are usually communications experts by a different name. Rarely do they have the clout to instigate real operational change.

In his book *Brand Resilience: Managing Risk and Recovery in a High-Speed World*, Deloitte consultant Jonathan Copulsky addresses the issue of ownership, specifically of reputational risk:

> "Increasingly, the Chief Risk Officer owns the measurement and tracking component of reputational risk. The bigger question is who's on the hook to address reputational risk challenges once they arise? That's where things get tricky. Because reputational risk is an enterprise issue, there is no

single person who can be accountable for it. That means the CEO, board and CRO are all ultimately accountable. It's a top-line imperative for most organisations today."

I would go one step further and question who is responsible for putting actionable plans in place to mitigate reputational risk *before* it arises. I strongly advise putting one person in charge of reputation and the reputation strategy, but agree with Copulsky that the cross-functional nature of reputation means that you need commitment at an enterprise level. The importance of reputational risk has increased so rapidly that a carefully formed steering committee can be used as a fast track to company-wide acceptance and understanding of its importance.

Over the past few years (since the advent of social media), communications experts have found themselves needing to keep their fingers in many different pies throughout the business. A single mishap by anyone in the organisation might damage your reputation, so somehow you have to ensure that every interaction with stakeholders is faithful to the strategy (and therefore to your company purpose and values). Equally, every interaction has the opportunity to be a reputation-enhancing experience.

The best way to approach this and to get buy-in is to involve representatives from all the groups that matter on the steering committee. You need active help from high and wide in the organisation. Gather the big battalions first. I suggest you include on the committee the most senior representatives from sales, IT, R&D, marketing, operations, finance, customer service, HR and legal.

The initial meeting should include an explanation of why reputation management has become a critical, board-level issue, illustrations of the potential impact a mishap could have on each area of the business and a confidential brainstorm to share thoughts on where vulnerabilities within each of these areas lie.

The meeting must be chaired by you, the CEO, though you might want to bring in an outside facilitator. It goes without saying that someone from your communications team should be deeply involved – you may want them to drive the meeting. But do **not** let committee members leave with the assumption that all actions lie with the communications team.

Reputation steering committee first meeting: Draft agenda

- **Process and behaviour** – examples from attendees of processes and behaviour within the business already supporting (or detracting from) reputation.

- **Reputational risk** – each attendee to highlight the single biggest issue within their own area that, if it spread publicly, could damage the company's reputation.

- **Social media** – ask if all (or any) are using social media, or even monitoring social media as far as is relevant for their role.

- **Insights** – share a breakdown of what is being said and the perception that exists online.

- **Brainstorm** – what are the behaviours and processes that best support our values and how do we use social media to amplify these?

- **Actions and accountability** – what actions will result and who is accountable for them?

Encourage each committee member to appoint someone in their part of the organisation to take responsibility for any actions the team sets them in its deliberations – this person will become an internal ambassador for reputation.

Ideally, you would have all senior managers in the business – from those departments mentioned above – contributing to the creation of the initial strategy, but in reality the presence of one or two of them should enable the committee to form a compelling strategy and, ultimately, a plan that people will accept.

Ask the steering committee to meet quarterly. There are two sides to this regular meeting. First, you need to continually get input from the committee members to the strategy. Second, each member of the committee is accountable for taking action within their division to contribute to the reputation strategy (so progress is being measured). They must all report back on successes and failures. Ultimately what's needed is to create some form of dashboard to demonstrate reputational risks and opportunities. The key is that each member of the steering committee contributes to the plan and its measurement.

WHAT SUCCESS TYPICALLY LOOKS LIKE

Let's say that using the planning process I have outlined in this chapter you have arrived at very clear goals for your desired reputation. You've defined your team's objectives and the key things you want to measure. You have communicated these across the organisation and believe there is broad buy-in.

There will almost certainly be reputation-oriented training for all senior managers to explain why it matters and to have information cascaded throughout the company.

You will also probably want to make changes in the customer service and key account management teams. You will have to make some of these quickly to avoid potential threats that you have uncovered. If you are a consumer-focused business, the strategy will undoubtedly integrate social media channels into customer service processes, for example. Even if you sell to other businesses, you may find that your target audiences are much more present in social media channels than you anticipated, perhaps because you are now listening better.

Having a reputation strategy in place will inevitably encourage an acute awareness of all contributors to reputation – from the greeting given by the receptionist to the quality of the end-product or service. Each and every customer and employee interaction needs to be completely and consistently in line with your core values, and the activity and behaviours outlined in your strategy and subsequent action plans.

Your communications team will have clear success metrics that go beyond the advertising value equivalents for media coverage (a formula whereby editorial coverage is given a monetary value based on advertising rates). They will look at the real benefit of the strategy to the company; looking at outcomes rather than outputs (which will be discussed later in the book).

Despite all these indicators, the true sign of success will be what your gut tells you. When purpose, values and behaviour are aligned, and communications are going well, you don't actually need metrics to know that what people think about you is generally positive!

Case study – reputation is worth more
than short-term costs

Teekay is a global energy shipping company headquartered in Canada. CEO Peter Evensen has strong views on the key drivers of corporate reputation and the role that social media has to play in it:

"What I tell all our people is that everybody has a say in the company's reputation. This includes the customers, the suppliers, the investors... anyone who comes into contact with our business. Obviously, employees can have the greatest influence in shaping it, so you need to start with making sure that what you say to people is consistent with what we say to ourselves, and most important, how we act. It all starts with corporate culture.

"You know, writing a letter and telling somebody 'we have a reputation for operational excellence', isn't going to cut it. You can't just talk about core values and a mission statement. You have to back it up. We always try to show people that we are consistent by what we do, not only what we say.

"Take safety. Naturally it is a number one priority in a business like ours. On some routes, Teekay has to be careful of pirates. Of course, the crew will be studying alternative routes – and as management we need to establish to what degree we are taking steps to ensure that they won't be put in harm's way. There are lots of things you can do – people always talk about armed guards on the ships, which is an option. But you could also reroute the ship to go on a longer, safer route. That can cost $30,000 a day, but in Teekay's view, an ounce of prevention is worth a pound of cure."

It is in its real-life incident training where Teekay has experienced the greatest impact of social media and today's changing communications environment. The company introduced a social media process into its training recently to see what the impact would be on the information flow. According to Evensen:

"We had this whole simulated social media exercise and we role-played an incident in Vancouver harbour. We sat and responded and made real-time decisions – should we respond to that? Is that real information? Is that accurate information? That was a real eye opener for me. I'm starting to understand the way a social crisis unfolds. We re-did our crisis management planning to ensure that we monitor and respond via social channels in addition to more traditional avenues. It emphasizes the fact that we have this idea that you only provide information when you know it to be absolutely right. Social media is fundamentally changing that aspect of how we operate our business. We need to get comfortable with the fact that we – as a business and the industry as a whole – need to share information as we have it, without the delays that are inherent in the fact-checking process. Information will be spreading whether we contribute to it or not. At least we can ensure that what we say is as accurate and up to date as possible."

The next few chapters will go into more detail about understanding your audience, finding your own company's voice and crafting compelling messages.

CHAPTER 10

Who Are You? Identifying Your Company Personality

THE HUMAN FACE OF
BUSINESS

Once you have the strategic process broadly mapped out and understand your reputation goals, it is really important to ensure you are clear on your brand's personality. This was less important several years ago, but the broad use of social media now means that people's expectations have changed. They generally expect businesses to have a more human face, while still offering a professional product or service.

This chapter will look at how you identify your company's personality and use it to your advantage. Ultimately it comes down to messaging – what is it you want to be saying to the outside world?

SEEING YOURSELF AS
OTHERS SEE YOU

These days, expectations are not only that people see businesses as responsive and customer-focused; businesses are increasingly being judged on likeability. All of this is, of course, in addition to your product or service being great. So how do you work out what you should be saying and what your company's personality is?

Whether you like it or not, your company already has a personality. It exists as a result of your culture and is reflected by the people who work for you in everything they do and say. You, the business leader, have been the principal influence on what that culture is.

Here's a quick way to identify the current personality of your business.

Take a piece of paper and write down the words that spring to mind when you think of your business as a whole. Don't choose the predictable descriptors like "customer-focused" and "innovative" (these are business attributes and may be relevant later on) – think about personality traits; for example, reserved, formal, serious, light-hearted, witty, inquisitive, curious, determined. List as many as you can think of, then repeat the exercise with your steering committee. Then ask your receptionist, your IT department, your HR department. You get the idea. Finally ask your suppliers and even some trusted customers to think about your company and do the same exercise. See if any words consistently emerge. I would be amazed if they didn't.

Ideally, choose three that emerge most frequently and also express what you yourself would want to emphasise. These aren't your core values, but they describe the personality of the business. For one large B2B client of mine recently we settled on passionate, professional and friendly. Once agreed, this personality should be reflected in ALL communication and interaction – inside and outside the business. It becomes part of the hiring scorecard and can be used to inform the tone of things like LinkedIn discussions, blog posts, your website and even your annual report.

If there is a discrepancy between the keywords that emerge from the exercise and what you want your business to be recognised for, you need to review your core values and your culture and work out what needs to change.

Next, think carefully about your target audiences – list all of them. These will be customers, prospects, employees, shareholders, government bodies, academics, potential recruits – name whoever is important to you. When you have your list, go through each audience and force yourself to determine who the top three are. You do this because no business can be all things to all people; you need to focus. In most cases there will be a halo effect emanating on to the other audiences you want to reach anyway.

Go back to the answers the three target audiences gave to the questions about personality you asked earlier. If by chance the three main audiences you have just identified were not part of the exercise, do it with them now. This gives you an accurate view of what your important target audiences think of you today.

Compare this with what you would like them to think. Hopefully, this will tie in with the answer to what you want to be known for that you have already worked out in Chapter 9. If it doesn't, perhaps you need to take a closer look at how your business is addressing the needs of your important target audiences. The emphasis here is on *how*. It's not what you are supplying to meet the target audience's needs but how you are doing it that concerns us.

Finally, check if there's an obvious clash between your business's personality and the target audiences you want to be communicating with.

SETTING YOUR COMPANY'S TONE OF VOICE

The tone of voice reflects the personality of the business. Look at the three words you settled on for your brand's personality; in most cases these will translate quite easily into your brand's tone of voice. A good definition of your tone of voice will provide guiding principles for anyone communicating on behalf of the company, using any medium. It influences the design of your print and digital media and templates in letters, proposals and advertising materials. In fact, the aim is to get the tone of voice to dominate any contact a stakeholder has with your business.

Suppose you settled on passionate, professional and curious as your business's personality, then use these words as the main driver in terms of what you are communicating and how you are communicating it. Ask surprising questions that offer insight to those who are connected with you. Or maybe your brand's personality is irreverent and challenging. If so, you might want the tone of voice to be witty.

If you have a content strategy (and I would highly recommend that you do), the three personality words and the tone of voice should be central to it. We have said that you cannot set a reputation strategy without understanding the business's purpose, values, vision and goals. In support of this reputation strategy, we have derived your business's personality and tone of voice. In the same way, editorial planning, or content strategy, must reflect deep understanding of your customers and support your business objectives. It is critical to align what you are saying and how you are saying it with the audiences that you are communicating with. In the next chapter we will look at understanding your audiences.

The three personality words and your tone of voice are useful in many ways as a guideline for communication. Use them as part of the training for your internal brand ambassadors, the people taking the lead in giving your reputation strategy a voice. Reinforce your company personality when briefing new employees as part of your induction programme. In fact, new hires will have experienced your personality already, since it should be woven into the hiring process.

UNDERSTANDING AND COMMUNICATING YOUR WHY

I referred in Chapter 4 to Simon Sinek's golden circle model and here is where it really starts to come into its own: Sinek sums it up as "people don't buy what you do, they buy why you do it".

This is so much easier said than done. Telling people what and how you do things is a no brainer. The challenge is to look at the bigger picture and to communicate why.

Once you have worked this out, you are really getting somewhere: you have three words describing your brand personality; you have your core values; and you're looking at aligning company behaviour with both of these. The element that will really turbo-charge your reputation is defining your *why*. What is your business's purpose, cause or belief? The ultimate goal is not to make people buy what you have, but to make people believe what you believe (again using the Sinek theory).

Here's a concrete example. I recently worked with one of the world's largest cabling companies. Naturally, it finds that differentiation is a problem when the product it is selling consists of miles of cable built to exactly the same specification as the competition. In an attempt to differentiate itself from the competition and to increase its attractiveness to customers, employees and shareholders, the company decided to identify its *why*. It always existed so we simply facilitated the process to help it come to the surface.

It boiled down to the fact that at its most fundamental level, the company connected people and power. A natural and genuine extension of this was *improving people's lives by connecting them to power*. That gave us the *why*. The company then decided on a tone of voice or personality that was friendly, professional and passionate. With these two elements alone, people in the business have clear parameters about what to communicate and how. The next step is to implement this thinking throughout the company so that behaviour reflects the purpose, and it is reinforced by all aspects of internal and external communication.

A clear view of your purpose guides the behaviour of your people and all the communications of your company, so it's key. Believe me, getting to the *why* is not a short or simple process for most traditional businesses. I would suggest that you have someone facilitate these discussions. They act as a navigator through the process so that it goes ahead without the scepticism that often occurs in meetings that challenge the status quo. Facilitators are also in a position to reflect back to you what they are hearing and improve the quality of the outcome.

The next step is to build up the key messages that support your purpose. Once you have the purpose defined, you are likely to find that you have a lightbulb moment and very clear competitive differentiation begins to emerge.

Use the same technique that we used to define your personality. Choose three key messages that you would use to communicate about your business; don't forget to do it in a way that matches your company personality and reinforces your purpose. And then ensure you have proof to back each up – no more than three proof points per message.

A great example of a company that has done this well is TOMS shoes. It is obviously slightly special because its mission includes giving shoes away to impoverished children around the world. I have never worked with the company, but its messaging is so clear that I thought it would be a fun exercise to reverse engineer its messaging based on the process outlined here.

Thinking about TOMS' personality
and messaging

Looking at its website and listening to the founder, Blake Mycoskie, it's easy to derive the personality of the business: approachable, humble and passionate.

Its key message is that it is *transforming everyday purchases into a force for good around the world by giving one for one.* For each pair of shoes you buy from TOMS it gives a pair to someone in need, a child who can't, for example, go to school because they don't have shoes. So a child in the USA who has bought a pair of TOMS shoes knows that somewhere another little girl is going to school as a result of her purchase. It's the ultimate feel-good buy.

TOMS' purpose: we are in business to help change lives.

From the business perspective Mycoskie suggests that building a profit-making business that gives away a lot of its profits is better than a straight charity because its giving is sustainable in the long term.

Let's go back to the process we outlined earlier and look at the TOMS proof points. If we had to guess at TOMS' three key messages and related proof points, they could be:

Message 1: We are transforming everyday purchases into a force for good around the world.

- We've given 10 million pairs of shoes, in over 60 countries, since we started in 2006.

- Since the introduction of our eyewear range in 2011, 150,000 people in ten countries have benefitted from free prescription glasses.

Message 2: Our business is no longer just a business. It's a movement.

- Thousands of people hold fund-raising events in partnership with TOMS each year.

- We offer four separate community programmes to help people get involved: one day without shoes, world sight day, tickets to give and campus programmes.

Message 3: We have a sustainable business focused on creating jobs in the countries where we give away shoes.

- We are currently making and giving in Ethiopia, Kenya, Argentina and China.

- Within two years we will produce at least 50% of our 'giving shoes' in the regions where we give them.

- We are currently testing production in India.

TOMS Shoes has a Facebook fan page with over one million likes. It engages regularly and authentically with its fans, including initiating polls to get feedback on specific issues. It has 800,000 followers on Twitter as well as a YouTube channel with a huge number of subscribers and millions of upload views. Even before you start to look at engagement statistics, that is an audience of nearly two million people who are actively following the business and keen to hear what it has to say. I know many B2B businesses that would give anything to have an engaged audience half that size.

Give concrete examples

Are all three topics – your personality, your purpose and your tone of voice – concrete enough for your people to understand and put into practice? Always give examples of what you mean in any training or other communication document that describes them.

QUICK REFERENCE GUIDE

- Make a list of personality traits that you believe describe the personality of your business. Reduce to three. Reflect these traits in all communications.

- List target audiences. Choose three key audiences. Compare what they think of you now with what you defined as your aspiration in the reputational strategy.

- Define your why/purpose.

- Express three key messages that support your purpose in a way that reflects your personality.

- Define three proof statements for each key message.

CHAPTER 11

Understanding Your Audiences

THE INCREASING POWER
OF KNOWLEDGE

There's nothing new about the need for businesses to understand the audiences that are important to them. It's the starting point for Dale Carnegie's classic *How to Win Friends and Influence People* and numerous other management tomes. The principle is that any pitch starts from the listener, not the presenter. We're selling, not telling. The customer's perspective must always remain in the spotlight.

As we think about our reputation in today's social media-driven age, the same principles still apply. However, the opportunity to put them into practice exists in a more public, and potentially more impactful, way. Every tweet and every blog post has to start from an understanding of the audience, and you and your company will be judged on how well you do this. The audience will react based on how you act in the first place and then how you respond to interaction.

This is a blessing, because it allows a business to amplify positive principles that will ultimately win friends, influence people and drive sales. But it can be a curse if your people and your business inadvertently (or knowingly) display the types of behaviours and attitudes that put people off. On social media platforms such off-putting interactions include being over-critical, condemning others and, of course, focusing too much on yourself. Basically, it's the same behaviours that would be off-putting in the real world.

The best salespeople have always understood the power of empathy and appealing, genuinely, to your audience's needs, urgent or otherwise. In today's world, the opportunities to deeply understand the audiences that are most important to you are endless. For instance, the advent of big data means the possibility to use audience insights in a meaningful way is now a reality. According to Annabel Dunstan, co-founder of data driven engagement consultancy Question & Retain:

"In today's world you can't really afford to care about your client only at the end of the contract or electoral cycle. If content is king, data is God. There are lots of ways to get information (buzz monitoring, newsfeeds, research, pulse checks) but none are reliable or complete in isolation. It is the combination of different sources of data that will give you the greatest insight. Asking for feedback is good – and all feedback is good, even if it's bad (it gives you something to act on and manage your reputation, rather than letting others manage it for you)."

THE POWER OF
CREATING PERSONAS

As social media has the power to unlock such detailed insights into your audiences (employees, customers, prospects, shareholders, suppliers, whatever they may be), those audiences will increasingly expect you to truly know them as individuals, not as part of a segment. The question is, how do you approach a known customer market of (potentially) hundreds of thousands of people with a message that displays understanding of each individual?

A useful way to shift your business's thinking away from traditional marketing segments is to be more persona driven. This is where data comes in. Try this exercise. Choose an individual (fictitious but representative) from each of your target groups and build a persona around them. Gather insights about the target groups you have identified:

- What do they buy from you?

- How often?

- How do they buy? Online, in-person, or through a broker or reseller?

- Do they recommend you publicly?

- How often do they complain?

- If so, about what?

At this stage you can begin to look at your segments in a different way. Where once you might have targeted, say, women aged 25 to 35 with children, today you might have a group that represents people who buy from you at least once a month, or who buy a particular product, or who shop at a particular time. You see where we are going with this. When you have that top-line information, you can drill down into who those people are. You're looking for clusters and patterns that identify individual characteristics better than traditional demographics do.

There are many companies out there to help you do this. It's called data analytics and it's an essential skill in the reputation economy. It uses detailed analysis of the past to help you understand where to find your target markets – or even your new hires – in the future.

Traditional audience segmentation lets marketers identify groups by age, gender and location, to use just three examples. Behavioural targeting lets marketers aggregate information, such as responses to certain offers. The combination of the two lets the marketer predict what products and services will appeal to someone with specific attributes and history. Patterns begin to emerge. The more data you look at, the more interesting those patterns will be.

Practically speaking, you need to get to know your audiences with all the information you have to hand. Back to our fictitious persona: you know some of his or her buying behaviours, now let's look at the person more generally:

- Gender

- Age

- Job

- Nationality

- Time spent online

- Sites visited online (and why)

- Social networks they use

- Devices they use

- What type of content is important to them?

- How much time do they have to interact with you and your content?

- What do they get out of you and your content?

- How do they make purchase decisions?

- What is their role in the decision-making process?

- Any obvious pain points?

If you don't know the answers to these questions, there is no harm in identifying real members of the current target group and asking them!

Once you know in detail who these people are, it is not so difficult to go and find them on social media. The beauty of social media is that it facilitates detailed granular targeting with the likes of Facebook and LinkedIn ads, and Twitter's promoted tweets appearing only in view of relevant prospects.

Knowing your audience: segment and focus

The Airport Operators Association (AOA) wanted to improve and increase engagement with members as part of its mission for 2013 called Members First.

Since 2011, the AOA has significantly increased its public affairs and lobbying activity. It has augmented this focus by seeking to gain a better understanding of its members' priorities, using a regular monthly Pulse Check to gauge member views. With rapid reporting, the AOA team is now able to respond to immediate feedback quickly and decisively, and use the data to inform future strategy and tactics. This not only improves the AOA's engagement with the external agenda and stakeholders, it has also resulted in an enhanced member experience, as members' views are taken into account when delivering the AOA's programme of activities and communications.

Outcome

By collecting feedback, analysing the findings and, crucially, acting on the data, the AOA's membership engagement (as measured by response rates) has increased from 7% to an average of 18–20% per Pulse Check, within six months. With some topics, such as the AOA Annual Conference, response rates were even higher. AOA member's overall satisfaction has increased by 10% year-on-year and the recent AOA Annual Conference recorded an increase of overall satisfaction of 22% to 80% (up from 58% the previous year).

To supplement the feedback process, focus groups have been set up with members to share and discuss the findings and go further in understanding specific members' needs. The focus-group led engagement programme has hit a 67% response rate and equally high satisfaction rates.

One focus group attendee said: "An organisation that exists to represent the views of its members should make every effort to listen and to collect those views and this is exactly what these meetings seem to be achieving. I have been a member of the AOA for many years and have never before been asked my opinion in such a constructive manner. It is most refreshing!"

Darren Caplan, CEO of the AOA, added: "Using an online pulse check tool is proving to be an incredibly efficient and effective way of maintaining a regular dialogue with our members and keeping track of our external reputation. To be an agile membership organisation is critical to us – especially one where our members are heard and we are seen to be acting on the feedback."

CREATING COMPELLING CONTENT TO INSPIRE YOUR AUDIENCES

Now that you know who your audiences are, what influences them and where they hang out, you can start to think about creating content that will appeal directly to them. This section is about the tone and substance of compelling communication. As you read it, however, don't forget that persuasive communication starts and ends with the receiver. In the end, you and your company exist to solve customers' problems by supplying excellent products and services. Offline campaigns and social media are there to help you to do that, so make sure you use them in a compelling way.

The topic of content raises another really important factor in the reputation economy and that's *generosity*. Building your reputation takes time and it is based on a give-and-take relationship. As a business, you mustn't be afraid to give. What you give depends very much on your business, but the easiest (and often most valuable) thing to give is knowledge.

The research we mentioned earlier from Edelman sets a fine example of this generosity. Undertaking and sharing regular research creates and builds relationships. Many businesses would view this as rather dangerous, giving its competitors insight into what the company is doing and where its focus lies. But I believe it's a sign of confidence. The Edelman team gathered the data, knows how to use the data and gets benefit out of it, so why not let others have a try as well; it's almost disdainful. I like it.

Tony Hsieh of Zappos gives tours of the business to anyone who wants one. They even brand it as the 'Zappos tour experience' and use it as part of their own marketing. There was a time in the not-so-distant past when this would have been unimaginable.

The founder of the business I now own used to have a mantra. He'd say "to be a market leader, the business needs to do the things that market leaders do." This holds true today. Gone are the days where companies held all their cards close to their chest. Today, the currency of reputation is built on trust and transparency.

An important part of your reputation strategy must be a well thought-through content strategy. What are you going to create that your target audiences are going to want to consume? The possibilities are endless of course. You could talk about your own or other people's research, or draft opinion pieces on topical issues around legislation or industry trends. You might want to run a top tips column or create a micro-site that serves as a one-stop shop source for information on a relevant topic. Whatever it is, it must be non-promotional and designed to genuinely help your target audiences with a specific challenge they are likely to be facing. This is equally true of the new mother who can't see the forest for the trees when it comes to choosing a car seat, or the harried senior executive who knows he should be doing something about moving his services to the cloud but hasn't the time to reflect on how to make that switch a reality.

The content you create must be credible and seen to be coming from you; but it doesn't necessarily need to be talking about the sector you are in. For example, the Dutch accounting software company Exact wanted to launch its cloud-based product in the UK, a market where the brand was completely unknown. In order to generate interest in the business, it aimed to create compelling content that would appeal to both accountancy firms and entrepreneurs running small businesses. It knew it didn't want to simply say, "We're here and we offer cloud-based business software, so give us a try."

After lots of research into its target audiences, the company decided to use a research-driven approach for its UK launch, creating content that would be of genuine interest to its target customers – small business owners and accountants. It commissioned a survey of 450 accountants and business people, looking at a number of business issues from both perspectives, and comparing the responses. As part of the research, the company found that £3.7 billion pounds were being lost collectively in the UK as a result of businesses simply forgetting to invoice. To distribute this content, the company used a combination of its own social media feeds and blog, traditional media relations, and direct outreach to accountancy firms.

This approach is fairly well proven. However, the difference with Exact is that the content was so compelling (and non-commercial) that more than 100 accountancy firms in the UK used the research on their own websites. How's that for a door opener in a new market? This is an example of good citizenship, good advice and good publicity – all excellent ingredients in developing the right reputation.

As you and your team think about the content strategy, it's important to bear in mind your reputation strategy. In doing so you must identify a central question that you want the content strategy to contribute to. Your reputation strategy supports what you want to be known for. The central question asks: "What are we trying to do, specifically with how and what we communicate?" Answers could include:

- Spark conversation – use a contentious tweet to get people fired up or pose a provocative question in a relevant discussion group on LinkedIn.

- Reinforce our expertise – develop a forum that demonstrates, shares and expands our expertise, perhaps a technical Q&A with experts on hand for free advice.

- Position ourselves as the employer of choice – create a programme specifically focused on entering and winning workplace awards.

- Demonstrate our innovation – publish our new ideas evaluation process and one or two of the ideas going through it.

Continuously reflect on the central question relating to a campaign. It can and should change frequently. But having it will help you distinguish opportunity from distraction once you start to get inbound interest, and also help you set clear measures.

Once you have decided what the central question is that you would like to address, it becomes easier to determine what sort of content you should create. And perhaps more importantly, where *not* to waste time and resources. For example, if your focus is on demonstrating innovation, perhaps you could create a series of videos giving a behind-the-scenes look at your laboratories, offering deep insight into little innovations that make a big difference.

Or maybe you organise a media visit to your most impressive R&D centre. Or you conduct research that looks at the greatest innovations of all time and turn it in to a coffee table book for your customers. Or you might create an innovations Pinterest board or Instagram feed and profile it on your site. And you could ask guest bloggers to contribute to your blog – ideally people who are known for innovation themselves.

If you are trying to spark conversation perhaps you could use your Twitter feed or Facebook page to ask thought-provoking questions. You might share stories that relate to your sector with a provocative question at the end. You might submit opinion pieces and letters to the editor that raise topics for debate, while having a strong opinion yourself. Or perhaps you could have spokespeople from your business contribute to other people's blogs. You could organise a panel debate with a journalist, you and other experts in your field, addressing the single biggest issue affecting your customers today. And the list goes on.

Show examples of successes. Remember the power of peer review. It may be inappropriate to actually quote a satisfied customer but you should certainly include the benefits that your innovation has brought to many people. It must be there, but it is important that it is part of a broader discussion on innovation. If not you simply appear to be broadcasting, which in the social media world is the same as showing off (and lacks the humility to make you likeable).

A good content strategy:

- Defines how you will use content.
- Meets business goals and satisfies priority audiences' needs.
- Guides decisions about content from creation to deletion.
- Sets benchmarks against which to measure the success of your content.
- Facilitates planning for the creation of useful, usable content.
- Covers not just what you're going to publish and where, but why.

A content strategy isn't just deciding what you're going to include. It's deciding what you're going to leave out. Avoid cliché. Try to make your blog, Twitter feed, YouTube channel, Google+ or Facebook page stand out from the others in style as well as content. Don't hold back from being controversial. Global interconnection and the massive database of information that the internet has assembled contain a lot of stuff that makes sense... and a lot of garbage. Make sure you're adding to the former, not the latter!

And finally, remember, great content:

- Tells your story.
- Answers people's questions.
- Inspires, entertains and motivates.
- Drives decision-making.
- Manages expectations.
- Brings your brand to life.
- Builds trust (but remember, poor content breaks it).

INCONSISTENCY WILL KILL
ALL YOUR GOOD WORK

With a content strategy in place you've reached the starting line. What matters most is that you are consistent and stick to it. Summarise it on one page and distribute it to anyone who will be contributing to external communications (why not all staff?).

It must be flexible enough for you to remain nimble and responsive if circumstances call for it. If, for example, there is a significant global crisis or a competitor makes a major move that renders your content inappropriate, you need to be able to get your content down fast, and other material up just as quickly to replace it. It's easy to think of examples of sportspeople who were closely linked to many commercial firms and products, but who have become involved in match fixing, drug taking and even criminal trials. Their sponsors had to sever ties as quickly as they possibly could, even if only temporarily.

Consistently doing things right

"If we consistently behave in the right way, our reputation will take care of itself."

Antony Jenkins, CEO, Barclays Bank

However flexible you have to be, remember that it's consistency that builds reputation (did you know that the Coca-Cola contour bottle was first sold in 1916?). If you continually do what people expect you to do, you will build up the goodwill that money can't buy. That applies to the content you create and the way you behave.

In getting the message across externally, here are the important questions:

- Do we know everything we can know about our most important stakeholders?

- Who is responsible for gathering and analysing this information?

- Are we applying it in all of our communications so that we know content is relevant and communications channels are accurate?

- Do we have a content strategy?

- What is the central question we are trying to address with our internal and external communications campaigns?

- Are we making the most of our content, online and offline?

- How do we know what content is resonating most with our important audiences?

Don't subdue genius

Don't let consistency stifle local creativity. The Chief Reputation Officer's job is to agree a company-wide content strategy that offers opportunities to be innovative and sparkle and even from time to time go off-message locally – geniuses make their own rules. You just need to ensure that your purpose and values are being upheld at all times, without exception.

ASK YOUR TEAM...

- With all the data available today, are we using it to truly understand our target audiences?

- Do we summarily disregard social media as a channel for our audiences, without knowing for sure if they are on there?

- What could we do in the next 60 days to get a better understanding of our target audiences?

CHAPTER 12

Crafting
Consistent,
Passionate
Messaging

A STORY
ONLY YOU CAN TELL

Now you have gathered such great detail about your various audiences this creates a real challenge when it comes to messaging. You have to balance producing a message that is totally relevant to one small segment with having a message that presses several buttons at a high level. In many ways, this challenge is one for the marketing department, integrating closely with your Customer Relationship Management (CRM) strategy. The objective is to develop a communications capability that allows you to communicate to many people, saying the most compelling things to exactly the right audiences at the right times.

But let's talk first about the message at the highest level. What about the elevator pitch, that now needs to be something more akin to a Twitter pitch? *What's your story in no more than 140 characters?*

It's something I've thought about a lot and indeed have faced myself in writing the *Playbook*. By now, you'll have realised that my message here, my elevator pitch if you like, is that purpose and values, supported by behaviours and consistent communication, builds reputation. That's the top line. You can choose to stop there, or you can choose to delve more deeply into the areas that pique your interest. It's the same with your business and its elevator pitch.

As a business you must have a single message that works at the highest level and is a story only *you* can tell. You must also write it so that you can develop it to suit the needs of many different people.

This is an area that most frustrates me in the businesses I encounter. So much work is done on creating all-encompassing tag lines or important descriptors that they end up losing anything that is unique to the business.

Let me give you an example. Years ago a mobile telephone equipment manufacturer (that I did not end up working with and that did not end up using this line publicly) thought long and hard and eventually came up with: "Bringing mobility to a mass market." But that could equally be true of a low-cost wheelchair provider. Or a car company. Think about context and what is *genuinely* unique to you.

Study Twitter profiles; they should be good examples of companies expressing their unique advantages in a nutshell. Here are two on the subject of sheds, I won't name them to protect the guilty:

- Market leaders in producing high-quality timber buildings.

- Producers of top-quality timber buildings.

Not inspiring are they? (Now's a good time to look at your own Twitter profile if you have one, just in case.) It's not that they aren't true, but there is simply no indication that these companies do anything special that would make me choose them. I know nothing about sheds, but if I wanted to get someone to build me one I might want to hear about the fact that they use only sustainably sourced wood. Or that they are the fastest. Or that they have architectural backgrounds. Or that they have a satisfaction guarantee. You get the idea.

You will find that your reputation strategy will help to drive the top-level message. You should also reflect on where you are with your reputation-building. Are you building? Maintaining? Repairing? The high-level message must accurately reflect the appropriate context or you will end up like the Canadian telecoms companies we looked at earlier who were trying to exploit virtues that their audiences knew perfectly well didn't exist, when they should have been working hard on repairing their reputation in time to take the new competition on.

BE AUDIENCE-SPECIFIC

In Chapter 10 you identified your three most important stakeholders (by the way, I really hope employees are in that list, given everything that we've said about behaviour and the potential to create ambassadors). The challenge now is to come up with a series of messages that work at the highest level, pique the interest of your audience and encourage them to engage further.

When it comes to social media, these messages can (and should) be tweaked to support the specific audience you are talking to. For example, an update you post on the private Facebook page for employees will be quite different from the discussion topic you post on a relevant LinkedIn group, aiming to trigger debate – even though they are on a similar topic. There is no benefit in repeating messages across the different media.

Don't get too worked up about the scale of potential audiences. Yes there are millions of people you could hit in various audiences, but focus on the top three audiences and you'll be well on your way. Explosive growth into other areas can always follow.

At this stage it might benefit you to take a look at the market landscape where you operate and see if there is any white space which is not currently occupied by you or a competitor, and that aligns with your purpose, values and behaviour. Conventional wisdom says that those businesses that appeal to a very specific target audience do best. Is there a particular target group that you serve really, really well?

Look for what it is that's different about the way you work and that sets you apart. For example, if the typical lead time in an industry is four weeks, could you do it in three? Or perhaps your customer service is second to none but you just take it for granted and are failing to use it as a lever for growing sales. What is it that you do that sets you apart when it comes to customer service?

Your messages need to be specific. They shouldn't be tag lines. You may use humour further down the communications line but I usually wouldn't recommend it at this "Who am I and what can I do for you?" level.

Your audiences don't need clever language. Think about what you would say at a cocktail party to describe what your business does in a sentence. I'll give you an example with my own business. For years I used to say that I owned a PR agency serving businesses in the science, engineering and technology sectors. Firstly, that all sounds a bit boring. But more importantly, it never really got to the crux of what we do and how we do it. Today, I just say "We make companies famous, among the audiences that matter most to them." It's not our tag line but it is a key message. And it can be easily reinforced both by telling people about the brands we've worked for, or by demonstrating specific contributions we've made to our clients' businesses.

Don't be tempted to try and be all things to all people. In the early days when we first launched Skype and asked about target audiences, we repeatedly heard "It's aimed at everyone." It might be true, but a key message that is so general is very hard to make compelling. What we ended up doing was creating specific campaigns aimed at certain audiences and working out related key messages. Audiences included grandparents (stay connected and see your grandchildren for free), expatriates (keep a close connection with home and avoid racking up a huge phone bill) and small businesses (great collaboration tool for distributed teams – avoid the email onslaught).

Keep your messages simple. When you think you have them, test them on people within your industry and those outside of it. If they don't get it, don't use it! A key message should not need a lot of explanation, but it should prompt audiences to say "Tell me more."

FINDING THE RED THREAD
THAT KEEPS
EVERYTHING CONNECTED

You need a red thread throughout the messages that you deliver to different people for different purposes. What I mean by this is the single unifying message that works throughout all your communications. It's not your elevator pitch – that would be too long. In fact it could be a single word or short phrase. Going back to Skype, the red thread was *free*. So although you are targeting messages at specific audiences, you are also being consistent in what you say. Look for it in your purpose, your values and what you say you want to be known for. It won't be hard to find.

This is particularly important in large businesses that address multiple sectors. For this type of company it will often come down to how you do something (simply superior products or outstanding customer service) or the two most common reasons businesses buy from businesses – because it saves them time or it saves them money.

Creating corporate messaging is nothing new. But what should be new for you is ensuring that these messages now accurately reflect the *why* in your business as well as the values. Looking at your values is a great starting point for your key messages (and remember it is your role to make sure all of this is backed up by behaviour that tells the same story).

Remember in Chapter 10 I suggested you ought to have no more than three key messages and, for each of those, using no more than three supporting proof points. We looked at the example of how TOMS may have gone about this. As you put these together, you should be thinking about your three key audiences and it might be that you mix and match what you say to support the overarching message based on which of the audiences you are talking to and what will most move or interest them.

A few questions to ask:

- Today, do your key messages reflect a story only you can tell?

- Do your messages support your core values?

- If an outsider asked five different people in the company what your key messages are, would they all say broadly the same things?

- Why are your people passionate about what they do?

- What do you believe about your business, your industry, your future?

WHAT MAKES YOU DIFFERENT FROM YOUR COMPETITION?

Creating differentiation is a perennial problem. For many large, well-established businesses it's a particular challenge because of the way they have been built up. If you were building your business today, with today's technology resources available to you, you might well do it in a very different way. It's why so many traditional industries are ripe for disruption by the small, agile and tech-savvy start-ups emerging on the scene today.

Many businesses get stuck when they think about differentiation because they think they must create something new. But as we looked at in the last chapter, the answer may lie in how you already do things today. In fact if you have survived for a time in a competitive market, it's almost certainly something you're doing now that is your differentiator. If your product or service isn't particularly unique (and there are very few that are), how you position it must be. Look at your values and your behaviours. Think back to the Zappos case study. Selling shoes isn't unique, but delivering truly outstanding, personal service for an online shop remains so today, despite the fact that Zappos started in 1999.

Having a clear purpose (or *why*) begins to come into its own at the messaging phase. Think back to Simon Sinek's "People buy from you because they believe what you believe" statement.

When it comes to messaging don't be tempted to get drawn into the *what* and *how* of what you do. Focus on what you want to be known for and the purpose of your business. A training company I know is a good example of this. It trains salespeople who sell technology – complex, big-ticket items to large organisations. It believes that the way to sell such products is to understand the customer's business and work out with them the return on investment that buying the product will bring. Its messages make this clear. Some companies believe differently. They think they need salespeople to be technically expert. When they ask for product training the company simply suggests someone else.

My company is similar. We believe that reputation is a business's single greatest asset. The clients who choose to work with us believe the same thing. If all they want is a press release factory, they go elsewhere.

As I've already said several times, it is equally important to communicate the belief and key messages internally, to ignite the passion within your employees. That way, every time they communicate (often on social media) the passion shines through.

Don't rush it, it's important

Take time to decide on your elevator pitch and red thread. The aim eventually is to create a consistent message about you and your brand that will last forever.

- What is our elevator pitch and how are we communicating it?

- Have we documented the proof statements behind our main message?

- Could our differentiation and red thread last forever?

CHAPTER 13

Handling a Crisis – Expect Disasters

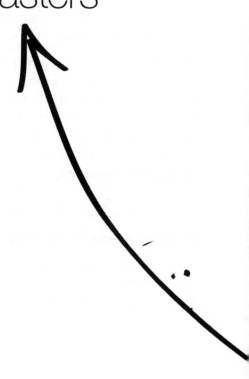

DON'T PANIC

Let's start with the formal definition of a crisis: a serious incident that affects human safety, business performance, the environment or product or corporate reputation, and has attracted or could attract adverse publicity. In my experience, it is this, coupled with the ability of social media to fan the flames, that keeps many CEOs up at night. And it absolutely must be addressed as part of your reputation strategy.

In social media terms, a crisis occurs when the story has escaped out of the company's control. For every company, the control threshold will differ. And the point at which negative social media commentary moves beyond mere noise to a more fundamental business issue will differ too.

There is no doubt that the media tends to overreact to social media flare-ups. It seems unfair that five people can create a crisis when they are offended by a brand and tweet about it. But journalists are always looking for news stories – and there's no better hunting-ground than social media.

That said, in my opinion it is pretty rare that the company under attack is the wronged party. Usually, something has happened that means it has failed to meet expectations. In short, a crisis can be triggered by something as simple as your product or service not being up to scratch. So although it's best not to panic, it is important to recognise a potential crisis for what it is and to act fast.

The impact of social media in highly regulated industries

Highly regulated industries have a particular challenge. For the most part, when things are going well, no one pays attention to them. But when disaster strikes, as in the case of the Fukishima plant in Japan, all eyes are on the company and every move is magnified. As a result, in industries like nuclear power, shipping and oil & gas, communications campaigns need to be split into normal operations and crisis situations. Getting the balance right is vital, so that the company or regulatory body builds up trust, transparency and goodwill during normal operations. Social media is having a significant impact on what, how and when these organisations communicate in both cases.

Particularly in crisis situations, information – often erroneous – travels at the speed of light. An analysis of the Fukishima disaster and the partial nuclear meltdown at Three Mile Island in the USA in the 1970s highlight the same issues; issues which today can and should be addressed in part by use of social media. There are three things that stand out as priorities:

1. Transparency in terms of productivity (what is happening to address the issue).

2. Transparency in terms of communications – providing information during a potential emergency when the event or status of a plant is not fully confirmed.

3. The relationship with, and role of, the regulator.

These three aspects severely coloured the aftermath and the perception of the Three Mile Island event, yet we saw the same issues at Fukishima some 30 years later. Social media has not only emphasised the significance of these three priorities, but may also provide part of the answer. If the companies involved in these disasters can move beyond the belief that information can only be communicated when it has been fully verified, it will be a great starting point. Information about an unfolding disaster *will* spread on social media. Having information from a reliable source that is the most accurate *at this time* is better than rumour and speculation.

This chapter emphasises handling a social media crisis using social media tools. But a crisis occurs when something has gone wrong and there is widespread knowledge of the error. Companies must put right the wrong or risk reputational damage, no matter what social media techniques they use. A major bank, for example, cited "reputational reasons" for blocking the redevelopment of suspected tax avoidance schemes. Another said it would no longer participate in transactions that breached its "tax principles". In both cases, removing the underlying problem was their chosen way of handling what was building into a crisis. Essentially using company behaviour to stop the potential crisis in its tracks.

Let's say you have a crisis brewing. *What do you do?*

MAKE SURE THE ALARM
GOES OFF IN TIME

Your listening system should first of all recognise the potential crisis and trigger the first step in escalating the problem to where it should be handled. News of a major crisis will inevitably reach you quickly in one of several ways. If the crisis has erupted offline, we may simply need to use social media as a listening and reactive mechanism.

Whether the crisis is being spread via social media channels at this stage or not, call together the crisis management team. This typically consists of members of the reputation steering committee, the communications team and a top manager from the function that sparked the crisis. It is key at this time that this group controls any communication that goes out from the company, so the rest of the company goes into communications lock-down. This must be part of your social media guidelines. Ideally it won't last long, but the last thing you need at this time is mixed or inaccurate messages being communicated.

However, one thing the whole company will be able to do is refer enquirers to a holding statement from the committee that they must get out very quickly. Based on all we've said earlier, it's important that the holding statement sounds human and commits to a regular update about the situation as it evolves (and that the team then delivers these updates).

Then it is time for quiet but urgent assessment while you work out the communications implications of what has happened:

- Which audiences are affected?
- How are they affected?

> "If you've actually done something unethical, then your best bet is to admit it, repent and promise to do better. It won't get you back to where you were right away, but people will tend to be relatively generous in their forgiveness to those who appear sincerely to regret having done something wrong and to atone for it."
>
> **Conrad Black**

There's a lot to be learned not only from businesses that are handling reputation well, but perhaps equally so from those who have handled it poorly. You need activity not only to put the problem right, but also to communicate messages that state what you are doing to correct and compensate for the poor performance. Ensure consistency of this message by briefing your people with a detailed Q&A document. Decide on the appropriate spokespeople by function and by channel. Remember to make the overall reaction completely aligned with the company's core values.

Tweeting an own goal: a social media crisis unfolds

In early November 2013 JPMorgan (JPM) announced on Twitter that it was hosting its first live Q&A on leadership and career advice, with a top executive from its firm tweeting answers to questions sent in by Twitter. The company teased who this would be a couple of times before announcing that in fact it was Wall Street legend Jimmy Lee, the "banker's banker" and JPMorgan Vice Chairman. At this point, and shortly before the Q&A was due to start, interest took off with the level of tweets going mad.

This tweet probably sealed the conversation's doom: "Hey look, @JPMorgan wants us to ask them questions under the hashtag #AskJPM! cc @StrikeDebt @OccupyWallSt @OccupyWallStNYC"

The resulting conversation was certainly not what JPMorgan had in mind when it conceived the Q&A idea. These three tweets will give you a taster for the others that came in:

- "Has the raw cunning of the electricity bid-rigging scheme been unfairly overshadowed by the scale of the mortgage settlement?"

- "Every time another person loses their home to an illegal foreclosure, does a bell ring?"

- "If it came out Jamie Dimon had a propensity for eating Irish children, would you fire him? What if he's still 'a good earner'?"

Not long after it started, JPM lowered its colours by tweeting, "Tomorrow's Q&A is cancelled. Bad idea. Back to the drawing board." To its credit, the final tweet was very genuine and did not try to hide behind any excuses.

The JPMorgan Twitter debacle raises several questions in my mind:

- Was a PR person (or anyone interested in company reputation as a whole) consulted on the plan to run the Twitter Q&A?

- What was the thinking behind using a senior executive who was not a regular Twitter user?

- Was any thought at all given to the reputational crisis the banking sector was going through, as a potential risk factor to the event?

Sure, hindsight might be 20/20, but these are things that must be considered when you enter into communications with audiences.

What is the role of social media in handling the crisis? Wherever news of the crisis started, you have to consider what's likely to happen in all the social media platforms. Information relating to the crisis will leak from one platform to the others so prepare a comprehensive approach. Identify your allies and ensure they are in the briefing loop.

The most important weapon in using social media to handle the crisis is your employees. The fact that you produced employee Social Media Guidelines as part of your social media plan comes into play here of course. At least everyone knows the basic dos and don'ts of social media. Brief them with the Q&A and consider empowering them to respond to relevant questions they are getting (even if it is to point people to an official social media feed) and they will eventually be the people who restore normality. The decision to do this requires an element of common sense and depends primarily on the gravity of the crisis. And it is only done once you have the relevant information with which to arm them. This approach will not be right for every business so you need to assess the potential risks.

Your general approach must obey the golden rules of crisis management:

- **Honesty** – don't use even the smallest falsehood to try to get out of it.

- **Transparency** – if you show people what you are doing you will set their expectations for improvement realistically. This is particularly true of timescale. If it's going to take a long time to get to the final solution be open and honest about that too.

- **Simplicity** – never, ever baffle your stakeholders with science.

- **Respect** – maintain respect, even for those who are disparaging.

- **Speed** – above all work fast. This will probably cost money and you must be prepared to spend it, but it's a smaller cost in the long run than taking a blow to your reputation.

You are going to have to manage very high emotions. People may be outraged. They may protest outside your premises. They may create a Twitter hashtag to help spread the negative message. How will you react if posts in social media start to suggest a boycott? Whatever the crisis, it's likely to escalate. So be prepared for the next wave of attacks, keep calm and respond. Keep up regular dialogue within agreed messages and ask followers to share content as it emerges. Respond fast so that the last string in a conversation is always yours.

You know that the impact will spread to other channels so be consistent and stay customer focused. One other thought – don't use online activity as an excuse for not talking to people directly. Quite often a problem with a single person or group of people might be best handled by a telephone call rather than by email or Facebook.

THE MORE I PRACTICE...

... the luckier I get.

This quote, attributed to the golfer Arnold Palmer, applies nicely to the handling of a social media-driven crisis. Practice. Get good systems in place. And listen. Make sure you hear the early warning signs. Don't forget to link to the feedback from all customer service channels – you may be getting bouquets from the mainstream of your users, but brickbats from a few, so pay close attention to them.

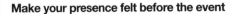

Make your presence felt before the event

"Some things quite quickly stand out, such as the need to build a presence. Because if there is an incident, obviously there is no time to build or establish a presence. You need to build the channel under normal operations so that it is there, and valued in crisis situations."

Carl Sommerholt, Director External Communications, Vattenfall Nordic

Social media is central to managing business continuity. Pre-prepared messages have their place in ensuring a fast response to difficulties. A scenario is a vision of an imagined or expected event. Scenario rehearsal is extremely useful in decision-making. If you can imagine something happening, you increase your chances of creating it or preventing it. Plot possible scenarios and rehearse your response. If you already do this, do you include social media response in your tests? Using scenario rehearsals also can help you gain insight into whether you are acting in line with your core values and beliefs. Use your processes to post appropriate video, comment and manage dialogue.

Have a plan B. You can't be sure that a crisis will not blow up while a key player is on vacation, so appoint and rehearse deputies. Research widely – other industry case studies may give you just the insight you need.

Remember to take cultural differences into account as you prepare your responses and dialogue. What seems like a sincere apology to a European may seem like rudeness to an American. Use your allies, give them a platform and let them be heard. Raise their profile; customers often help each other to overcome a shared problem. If one customer is helping another, use social media to celebrate this and reward them where possible.

Eventually the crisis will be over and you will have a lot of people to thank. Do so profusely. It pays to keep open the discussion threads that the crisis started for as long as possible – you still have the opportunity to learn from what is being said and if you are really lucky, you may end up with some ambassadors who praise the way the crisis was handled.

Transparency as we've never seen it before

"I don't think social media on its own is the silver bullet when it comes to restoring confidence in an industry. I do think not using social media – not responding to difficult questions or upholding transparency or dialogue – is just limiting yourself and will likely come up short in terms of stakeholders' expectations on responsive communications. The nuclear industry is a case in action. We need to work to uphold transparency and relentlessly inform the public about our normal operations. We should anticipate that civil society expectations on transparency will continue to grow, for us as well as for many other industries."

Carl Sommerholt, Director External Communications, Vattenfall Nordic

---

What do you do with negative comments? This is a very tactical question, but one I hear from CEOs time and again. The answer is, resist the temptation to delete them. Removing sites or pages has its advantages and disadvantages but generally it's better to leave material up there. It will eventually be replaced and forgotten and until that happens it's best to avoid the online accusation that you censor stakeholder feedback. Experiencing a crisis by definition is not going to be part of your plan; so do the crisis preparation well.

> **They'll follow your lead**
>
> Make sure that as leader, you exhibit calm and confidence to inspire your team to battle through tough times.

- If we are not active on social media, do we have a monitoring service in place? And if not, do we have an agreed supplier who will support us urgently should a crisis arise?

- What role does social media play in our business continuity/ crisis plans?

- To organise a rehearsal of a possible crisis scenario.

CHAPTER 14

Building Communities of Interest

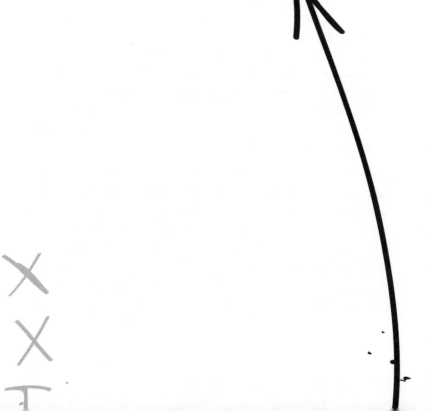

WHAT DOES IT MEAN AND IS
IT RIGHT FOR MY BUSINESS?

Aristotle apparently said, "Man is by nature a social animal," so it would be fair to say that social groups, tribes or communities are nothing new. Community-building in social media terms is more modern of course and has become a bit of a buzzword only over the past five years or so. But what does it really mean to you, the leader of a business, and how does it fit in with your reputation strategy? In short, do you need to worry about it?

Sean Hazell, head of brand innovation at Idea Couture, a strategic innovation and design experience firm, puts it beautifully:

> "Communities present both enormous threat and enormous opportunity for organisations. Declining to participate with people who are passionately involved in causes and conversations relevant to your company significantly increases your social susceptibility. Conversely, identifying community opportunities and championing causes your customers care about can earn loyalty, inspire innovation and act as a people-driven insurance policy. You look to the customer forums of the world's most loved brands and it's clear community advocacy makes for both great offence and defence."

Since the beginning of time people have gathered into groups that share a common interest, challenge or purpose – from health-based support groups, business groups based on industry or job, school-based groups, gatherings for new mothers, people who drink real ale and others who support the Toronto Blue Jays or the South African Springboks. People create these groups because they address a specific need – to share insight and information with a group of peers, in order to solve problems. But their first and fundamental appeal comes, as Aristotle said, from our human nature. We are social beings. That's what we need to bear in mind as we try to reach out to groups who are sympathetic, or even empathetic, with what we are trying to do – our *why*.

Social media platforms have created the perfect environment for individuals to find each other and come together to form groups and thrive. Political groups can propound a message, argue out the best approach to the voter and coordinate campaigns. Activist groups can provide care to people who need it on a regular or emergency basis, or organise a demonstration; the police can use the same media to monitor them. All of these things are already happening.

Employees can form various groups to assist a good employer to succeed and to protect themselves from bad employers. Customer groups can share experiences of the product and services they use. They can swap stories and spare parts, come together for conventions and make suggestions and representations to suppliers. It's quite possible that any or all of these types of groups could use social media as a community to help or harm your business with or without your acquiescence.

Understanding this community-based trend and responding to it will make you even more powerful in how you communicate with your stakeholders. But more than anything, existing communities provide an opportunity. They represent groups of people with a common interest – and if that interest is aligned with your purpose, there's no better group to talk to, learn from and share with.

> ### Community as innovation input
>
> "Today's social web is essentially the world's largest, un-ending focus group. And in today's always-in-beta environment, connecting with your most involved stakeholder groups serves as a critical real-time research input. Whereas traditional research methodologies often fall short contextually, community participation not only helps extract data and derive insights in the wild, it presents piloting opportunities and feedback on the fly. Among smart brand-builders, combining community listening, implicit observation, interpretation and participation is an increasingly common formula for customer-led innovation."
>
> **Sean Hazell, head of brand innovation, Idea Couture**

Having taken the audience insights which big data and the right analysis can give you, it is now a matter of defining how these communities come together. In some cases the opportunity may lie in creating the communities for people, offering them their chance to benefit from interacting with like-minded individuals.

In terms of reaching important stakeholders, we have talked so far about gathering data and drilling down through market segments in order to have the potential to undertake detailed, granular marketing. That process delivers information about groups of individuals who are of interest to us because they are aligned with our purpose and values, and are interested in our products and our services. Now we are thinking about identifying communities of individuals who might gather together, particularly on social media, for reasons we will identify. The task then is to engage with these communities, to learn from them, and to share with them the things that they might find most valuable.

When it comes to community-building, it doesn't just relate to customers. Your employees will undoubtedly form a community of their own too. In this domain, the role of the leader is to make sure that you are asking the right questions about the business's use of social media. It's important that you take stock of your business's own position in terms of the multitude of media and the scores of relevant posts, blogs and tweets that are out there.

WHAT DRIVES PEOPLE TO CONNECT WITH YOU?

What drives people into communities and why do they stay? In one instance people join a community because they have a pressing need. You may join a group when you have an illness, using forums, blogs and Twitter to share thoughts and news about treatments, or simply to be with people having a similar experience. When you have recovered you are likely to eventually leave; membership of the group has met your need.

Similarly if you have a security virus-derived problem with your computer you may well join a group concerned with countering that threat and then leave when your computer is clean. These are good examples of groups but probably not the ones you want to create or engage with your social media budget – you are looking for something more long term.

From Freud to Maslow and many others, psychologists have had their say on why, at a basic level, people join communities. For our purposes I've distilled them down into four reasons:

1. A sense of belonging.
2. A source of specific, relevant and potentially hard to access information.
3. The ability to connect with others who share a passionate belief (positive or negative).
4. The ability to work together to bring about change.

These groups can be extremely powerful and have the ability to change things. For example, a very active three-year social media campaign to stop UK resident Gary McKinnon from being extradited to the USA for hacking into Pentagon computers resulted in exactly the outcome Gary and his mother wanted.

Businesses need to understand how to tap into such groups in an effective, meaningful, sensitive way that will – most importantly – add value to the community members. Start with identifying communities that already exist and where your brand fits. Your contribution, apart from the possibility of very sharply targeted advertising, might be to assist with knowledge, access to experts, written materials or other content that adds genuine value to the group.

Community and complexity

"The principles of community are no different online or offline. However today's social technologies allow for unprecedented size, access and visibility. For businesses this means a more complex consumer culture to navigate; but it also means an opportunity for increased involvement. Today marketers have the power to identify what their products and services mean to the masses, alongside how they are relevant to very diverse sub-cultures. Being amidst the fragmented media landscape, following the many influencers on organisational reputation can be daunting. But the ability to map and monitor perceptions on a micro level also offers a unique bottom-up perspective to power cohesive company-wide strategy."

Sean Hazell, head of brand innovation, Idea Couture

Once you know the drivers that have led members to current communities you can start to think about how to fit into them or how to stimulate new ones. What could you genuinely offer individuals in a community of interest to you, as part of your own drive to further your reputation (based on behaviour)?

Once you understand the drivers of communities, you need to think about your strategy with existing communities relevant to your business. Think about both customers and employees, as well as suppliers and shareholders if appropriate. And focus on what you are trying to achieve with your reputation strategy. Does community-building fit naturally within it?

Here's a pretty basic example: a number of individuals have built up very vibrant online communities dedicated to triathletes. The community owner of any of these forums is likely to be an avid triathlete him or herself. The group talks about training plans, race day strategies, online resources, the latest kit and so on. These forums/communities are like gold dust to brands because they provide access to a select group of people who are interested and active in a specific area. For this example, think about sports technology providers, nutrition providers, people who sell online training plans – all very suitable for some relationship with this online community. But how do you connect with the group in a way that is real and won't be seen as spammy?

A San Francisco-based start-up, Linqia, has built a business to answer exactly this question. Linqia has a way to connect trusted brands with dozens to hundreds of community managers. Its technology identifies the most active communities across all social networking channels – blogs, Facebook, Pinterest, Instagram, Twitter, Tumblr and others – and matches the community leader with brands. Contribution from the brand is overt, but the system works because only relevant content is created by the community leader and shared with the group in an authentic and nuanced way. And it is the community manager – not the brand – who is in charge.

You will think about the obvious platforms today – YouTube, Facebook, LinkedIn, Twitter, Google+ and Pinterest.

But don't stop there. Some of the most powerful online communities exist in their own right. For example, Mumsnet, the UK's largest online community for parents, has 50 million page views per month. Or there's GrabCad, an open platform for engineers with nearly 1 million members. With thought and research your team will create a long list of communities that have a direct or tangential link to what motivates your customers and defines your products and services.

There are very big companies around the world that are doing this and doing it very well. Particularly for those businesses that have not yet engaged in social media, the opportunity exists to review how other businesses have handled it, and learn from their mistakes and successes.

Dell: measuring up

One of the ways that Dell measures the impact of social media on reputation is by using the Dell Social Outreach Services Team. It is responsible for identifying issues in social media and responding to them (via the @DellCares and @DellCaresPro handles). One of the key measures is whether it can shift the sentiment of the people it is dealing with. As part of its direct outreach, 50% of what it calls 'ranters' (people who are not happy with its products and services), were able to be shifted to 'ravers'. So of the customers who are demoters for Dell, 50% are switched to promoters. That's a really important measure for the company. It is clear that the social media activity has an impact on the relationship it has with its customers.

Dell uses a number of different programmes specifically to target different kinds of customers, who range from IT administrators, to developers and thought-leaders. One of these is IdeaStorm, which is an online community designed to help Dell listen to customer input. IdeaStorm also allows the customers to provide ideas to improve its products, services and, essentially, how it does business. That started back in 2007 and as of July 2014, Dell had over 550 ideas that had been implemented from that community, including the backlit keyboard, which many people will be familiar with. The company has had almost 20,000 ideas that have been submitted overall. Dell's customers go on the site and vote and comment on the ideas, or they post their own ideas. These are people who are fans of the products; they want to promote the product because they like the company, the brand. It's mutually beneficial, a real win-win.

One of the things that Dell has done which has been really successful is to create a training programme around social media to engage its employees. The company started it informally in 2007 and added some certifications around it in 2010. The programme helps participants understand what it is that they should be talking about in social media. Any employee can take the training and about 10,000 employees have been certified over the past three years. Those employees are then encouraged to go out on social media and speak on behalf of Dell, to actively advocate for the company. There are some rules that they all have to follow for that to be OK. For example, employees will always identify themselves as employees of Dell – in Twitter they'll use the #IWork4Dell tag. They are always very transparent that they work for Dell. They've done this in over 55 countries, and over 17,000 team members have completed at least one of the training programmes. Needless to say, the activity is backed up with a social media policy and governance and Dell has a social media lawyer on board as well. Layered on top of it is a really successful engagement model.

If you are going to create a community yourself you need to make sure that it is very tightly focused and that you find the right people to nurture it. Building trust takes time. People are sceptical of communities that are hosted by a brand or business that has a vested interest in creating it. Make sure the advice and information on the site is broad, impartial and accurate. Remember the basic need that drove people to join your community – a source of specific, relevant and potentially hard to access information.

PUTTING A COMMUNITIES-
DRIVEN PROCESS IN PLACE

Many businesses have an online community manager in place. This person is the main representative or ambassador of a company or brand on the web. The community manager creates and/or monitors communities generated in blogs, forums and other social networks. Ideally, this position should be filled by an employee, rather than outsourced to an agency.

In essence, a community manager is a full-time brand evangelist. This individual should be the most passionate person you can find about both your business and your industry. They must have a thirst for knowledge and they will be a force for good in your chief reputation officer's team. The individual *must* know your products and services inside-out and must also be able to educate people internally about the role of communities and social media generally. They must be able to look at the high level dashboard created by metrics from across the business and look for opportunities and risks.

This person will have their finger on the pulse of all existing social platforms and will be accountable for ensuring all social activity is in line with the content strategy and the reputation strategy. They might have a team, or they might use the resources of an agency. But the mistake I believe many companies make is in viewing this as a purely tactical, rather than an important strategic, role. It isn't. This person has enormous power not only to shape your reputation by the things they say online, but to give you insight into what your stakeholders are saying.

Putting a process in place for community management is unlike putting processes in place for many other things. There is a huge element of trust involved, which is why it is critical to get the right person for the job. Perhaps you should think of them as the mouthpiece for you, the CEO, because that's how the communities and readers of anything on your social feeds will see them. You can't ask for every tweet or post to be approved by a senior manager. That takes time and time is at a premium when it comes to online interaction. What the community manager wants to publish they publish. That's how important they are.

According to Dr. Konstanze Alex-Brown who leads Global Communications Social Media strategy at Dell, there are a few key things a CEO should think about when considering community-building:

- **Listen** – don't do anything before you listen. Go out there, get on the social media channels and understand the industry. Don't focus merely on your own company; take time to understand the pain points of the whole industry and understand the language your customers are speaking.

- **Never lose focus on the customer** – that's who you should be focusing on. You can't lose if you do that, that's what they want from you.

- **Go where your audience is** – make sure that you're going specifically to where they are, don't make them come to you. Go into the communities where they already exist; that's how you build momentum for what you're trying to do.

- **Be authentic** – particularly in the space of social media. You have to be comfortable that it's a part of your culture. The two go hand-in-hand.

- **Engage your employees** – if you want to be successful, empower them with knowledge on how to engage in social media, provide them with guidance and resources to be your best advocates. Then they can help carry your mission in their own way, with their own personality. They're really your best asset.

So, your process might be more like a flow chart, showing the community manager's touch points, identifying where they need to feedback to managers and identifying the best sources (internally and externally) for information. It should also include guiding principles. These will be different for every company but might include things like:

- Respond within one hour.

- Never blame the customer.

- Actions speak louder than words – always look for the potential to act.

- If in doubt, escalate.

Have a feedback loop in place

Encourage employees to feed back any relevant information to the community manager about the communities that they have involvement with.

ASK YOURSELF...

- Is each function in the organisation involved in communities centred around their function?

- Do all stakeholders understand how to tell the community manager about any online activity relevant to the success of the business and the importance of doing so?

- Do I meet regularly and informally with the community manager in my business? If not, why not?

- Could I be doing more to use social feedback to drive innovation?

CHAPTER 15

Communicating
Via Social Media

IS IT FOR YOU?

Gone are the days where businesses had to work exclusively through third-party gatekeepers called journalists. There are myriad ways to get your message heard directly, if you do it right. But tread carefully because if you get it wrong, you can do more harm than good to your reputation.

We are living in a time when information can spread further and faster than ever before. Get the values and behaviour wrong, and it's a matter of when you will be exposed, not if. But get it right, and the potential for social media to act as a loudspeaker for all the amazing stuff you are doing is tremendous. The best part is, if you get it right, your company won't be the one doing the shouting. It will be all the ambassadors you have created as a result of building such a solid and genuine reputation. It becomes a self-fulfilling prophecy.

Today's social media platforms have the potential to amplify your presence, but what's even more exciting is what the future holds. Who knows what sorts of communities might spring up – and in what way – to provide the perfect outlet to reach your target audiences. The good news is, if you have followed the framework I have outlined, then the channels won't matter. Whatever they are, your teams will be ready and able to spring into action.

WHY CONSIDER IT?

Most large multinational companies ticked a box several years ago and put social media guidelines in place. Now that people are tweeting, posting, reviewing and pinning around the clock, they need more than mere guidelines. Companies need to develop those guidelines into all-encompassing reputational strategies that manifest themselves in employee behaviour.

Just over 60% of those CEOs surveyed by Zeno Group in its digital readiness survey in 2012 believed that they could respond to a negative post or article within 24 hours. 24 hours?! By that time a digital wildfire could be well and truly underway, damaging the company's reputation beyond repair.

Add to that the following statistics relating specifically to B2B social media and we start to get a clearer picture of why it needs to be on your boardroom radar:

- There are three billion people online. Some of these will be your employees, customers and investors.

- In the USA, people spend on average an hour on their smartphones every day (talking, texting, and browsing the internet), and one-fifth of internet traffic now comes from mobile connections (Experian and Statcounter).

- 74% of B2B marketing companies use Twitter to distribute content (Content Marketing Institute).

- B2B marketers who use Twitter generate twice as many leads as those that do not (Inside View).

- For B2B companies, LinkedIn is the most effective social network, with 65% having acquired a customer through the professional network (Marketing Charts).

- Social media can improve relations with employees; 82% of employees say they trust a company more when the CEO and leadership team communicate via social media (eMarketer).

INFLUENCING THE DISCUSSION

Given such statistics, social media clearly has a role to play in how you communicate. But how do you best influence the perception of your business, and therefore protect its reputation, by your actions?

These actions might be online or offline, but commentary on your brand's actions will undoubtedly take place via social channels.

If you say one of your core values is to be customer-focused, are you sure you have a presence where your customers are? Does your customer service department know if people are complaining about you or your products on social media? Or are there people saying positive things about your business that you are unaware of? Do you have a plan in place and a feedback mechanism to answer complaints and other key questions?

When language reflects culture

"If you have amazing people in your team, and they give amazing service, people will do business with you. If you're bright enough to reinvest some of the business that's been generated by the customer back into the people that gave the amazing service in the first place, they'll actually give better service and you're strengthening your culture. Your colleagues will move from being committed to being loyal, and the same thing will happen with your customers. The glue starts to form. And as a result of that you have a company that becomes self-fulfilling."

Chris Brindley, MD Regional Banking, Metro Bank

Think about it – there may well be issues that are beyond your control, but if you know that public discussions are taking place it is well within your ability to comment on them in order to protect your own reputation.

I'll give you an example. One company I worked with years ago provided an essential component for large commercial aircraft. It had a longstanding contract with one of the two major aircraft suppliers. When one of the two companies (not my client's customer) experienced major issues, resulting in a fatal aircraft crash, the issue was initially linked to this particular component, provided by another supplier.

News began spreading fast. My client had nothing to do with the component failure, it had maintained its usual high standards. The company therefore had nothing to do with the plane crash, yet was being incorrectly linked with the story. This is a great example of the need to monitor and to be able to respond quickly and appropriately.

Stop thinking about how to control what the public is saying, because that's wasted effort, and start thinking about how you can influence it. The bad news is that instant access to social channels means that unhappy customers or embittered employees can air their dirty laundry; the good news is that it also means that happy customers or employees can share their delight. Doing nothing is not an option.

SO WHERE DO YOU START?

Below is a sample social media plan, to give you an idea of what it might include. It is a subset of the communications plan which is a subset of your reputation plan. It all fits together.

Sample social media plan

A social media plan will cover the following topics:

Current position

- Which stakeholders are involved in social media and, of those, which are the top three your social media plan will zero in on?

- Customers – their attitudes should primarily guide your social media activity.

- Which stakeholders have the most authoritative voice in achieving your social media objectives?

- How do you deal currently with media, journalists, commentators and influencers?

- Looking at the general levels of activity on all social media, what is the current position statistically versus competitors?

Objectives

- Primary objectives – could include increasing awareness of product/brand and driving traffic to a website, blog or hosted site.

- Secondary objectives – could include influencing influencers and promoting your company to internal stakeholders.

Tactics

- Once you have an understanding of the compelling content required, the types of conversations you will have with your audience and your tone of voice, then you need to start engaging in an effective way.

- Identify the central question.

- You may very well decide to share advice, experience and contacts with your audience.

- You may employ paid-for tactics hiring businesses or other personalities to create brand awareness, increase follower numbers and drive website traffic.

Channels

- Include the specifics you are going to use for all social media, for Twitter, forums, blogs, LinkedIn and so on.

Measurement

- Where sensible and possible include measures such as traction, traffic to blogs and websites.
- Don't forget to identify related *outcomes* you are aiming for.
- Give users opportunities to sign up for polls or surveys.

Employee Social Media Guidelines

- It should be part of this plan to compose simple guidelines for employees to use social media in a way that maintains consistency and adds to the company's ability to deal with crises and exploit social media as an aid to growth.

Once the decision to undertake any level of communication via social channels is agreed, you need to create some lines in the sand:

- What are the boundaries for action?
- Where are the legal boundaries, if there are any?
- How will you empower those managing the social channels to act in line with your core values? This might entail spending money.

Don't get the impression that this is all about giving away free stuff. It's more about being generous with knowledge, with your time and with actions to prove that your customers really do come first.

A good example of a B2B business doing things well is shipping company Maersk Line. Its customer panels are not unusual. What is slightly unusual is that it publishes them on its website, for all to see. Its Twitter feed is also friendly, frank and open – all elements that contribute to a positive reputation, particularly in times of normal operation in an industry that is well equipped to handle crisis situations.

Again, remember that in creating a social media plan, you're delegating authority to a bright person to act quickly and decisively in the company's interests. You're not abdicating responsibility for running your business. Put in place a plan to elevate an issue from media listening to management activity and an agreed timeframe for a response. (Hint: it must be less than 12 hours and ideally only one!)

BURYING YOUR HEAD
IN THE SAND

If this all sounds like too much of a headache, there is an alternative: just ignore social media altogether. If you're not taking part, it can't hurt you, right? If only...

There is a possibility, not a strong one I agree, but a possibility nevertheless that if you don't set up a corporate Twitter feed (to use just one example) someone else might.

A United Airlines (@UnitedAirlanes [sic]) parody account was created in May 2012 and tweeted for a month before going silent. More than a year later, the creator of the account realised people had been sending messages to him on the assumption that it was the official United Airlines Twitter feed. So, naturally, he blogged about it:

"Found out last night that for months, angry customers having been tweeting at my fake parody airline account,

United Airlanes, to bitch about their experiences with United Airlines."

From that point on, he began to reply to some of the people's complaints. Here are some examples of what people said and how the fictitious @UnitedAirlanes representative responded. For those readers who are not Twitter users, the conversation aspect of this might not be obvious. I have annotated to make it a little clearer. This was all conducted in the public domain:

[Customer @nffc65] This @unitedairlanes flight crew is incompetent can't load the; [sic] plane horrible service

[Response from fake United Airlines account] @nffc65 You should see our crews load a t-shirt bazooka though – Ralfio can in seconds. He can even hit business class from the cockpit!

[Customer @sarahlouisedob] @unitedairlanes is the true meaning of cattle class. Delays with no explanation. Food you should feed to the dog and staff that don't care!

[Response from fake United Airlines account] @sarahlouisedob Oh shit, did you eat the food? You're not supposed to actually eat the food.

[Customer @alexglaser101] it amazes me that after all the advancements in planes these days @unitedairlanes still has the worst entertainment system known to man!!!

[Response from fake United Airlines account] @alexglaser101 It's a missile made of gun metal traveling at fast [sic] through space there are few amenities available inside a giant bullet.

It is hard to believe that this was going on behind United Airlines's back. Or rather, right under its nose. If only someone had cared to look! This is just another example of why monitoring is truly essential. Sometimes what you don't know *can* hurt you!

Even traditionally conservative brands like Goldman Sachs are present on social media, not to mention the Pope and the Archbishop of Canterbury. It's interesting to see how the tweets from Goldman Sachs are about training, core values and businesses contributing to the environment as much as they are about supporting businesses and making money. Make of that what you will.

In a really insightful McKinsey report called 'Demystifying Social Media', the authors Roxane Divol, David Edelman and Hugo Sarrazin say:

> "In short, today's chief executive can no longer treat social media as a side activity run solely by managers in marketing or public relations. It's much more than simply another form of paid marketing and it demands more too: a clear framework to help CEOs and other top executives evaluate investments in it, a plan for building support infrastructure, and performance-management systems to help leaders smartly scale their social presence. Companies that have these three elements in place can create critical new brand assets (such as content from customers or insights from their feedback), open up new channels for interactions (Twitter-based customer service, Facebook news feeds), and completely reposition a brand through the way its employees interact with customers or other parties."

I couldn't agree with these sentiments more. The full report is on the McKinsey website (**www.mckinsey.com/insights/ marketing _ sales/demystifying _ social _ media**).

I am not advocating that all businesses must be active on social media, merely that your approach to reputation-building is thoughtful, and that you carefully consider whether social media could be a powerful positive force for your company. Take into account the possibility that your business's absence from social media could be a negative force. Can you afford not to talk to the millennials using their channels?

> "A survey of C-level executives suggested that their companies are using digital technology more and more to engage with customers and reach them through new channels. What's more, an increasing percentage reports that their companies are making digital marketing and customer engagement a high strategic priority. Nevertheless, there is more work to do: most executives estimate that at best, their companies are one-quarter of the way toward realizing the end-state vision for their digital programs."
>
> **McKinsey Global Survey**

In case there is any confusion, one area you must be active in is listening. You need to know if and when something critical arises on social platforms, and you need to have a plan in place to respond to it. You're doing this not least because it could wreck your business if you don't.

I am sure there are plenty of businesses where it makes sense **not** to be present in social media. The important thing in this case is that it is a conscious decision.

REPUTATION AT A GLANCE

Before we move on to look at getting the most from your spend on reputation, here's a reputation flow chart to remind you of everything we've covered in the *Playbook* so far.

REPUTATION FLOW CHART

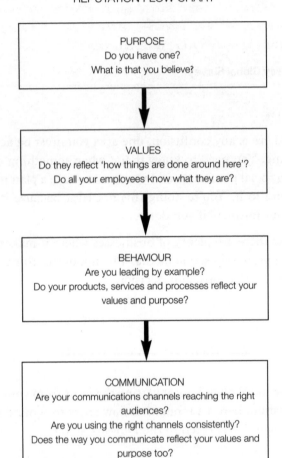

PURPOSE
Do you have one?
What is that you believe?

VALUES
Do they reflect 'how things are done around here'?
Do all your employees know what they are?

BEHAVIOUR
Are you leading by example?
Do your products, services and processes reflect your
values and purpose?

COMMUNICATION
Are your communications channels reaching the right
audiences?
Are you using the right channels consistently?
Does the way you communicate reflect your values and
purpose too?

Getting The Most From Your Spend On Reputation

I don't have an answer to the perennial issue of how to consistently measure the value of reputation. For all the reasons outlined in this book, the measure needs to be identified by you, in a way that is relevant to you and measurable by you. You need to identify a series of attributes that form an umbrella measure of how the world sees you. Such a measure allows you to work out where you are now and put in a monitoring system that plots the ebb and flow of your reputation.

This is not about measuring the success of social media or PR campaigns. It is about measuring the success of the business. If the business is doing well, it is a strong signal that your reputation strategy is working. In fact for some businesses, it is the *only* measure. Having said this, identifying key criteria and where the shortfalls lie is a really simple way to get an at-a-glance view of focus and progress.

These topics are the focus of Section Four.

CHAPTER 16

Measuring
Your
Reputation

A 2013 report by Weber Shandwick, 'Safeguarding Reputation', estimated that 63% of a company's market value is attributed to reputation. And not only that – research undertaken among CEOs for the report found that the average estimated time to fully recover from an issue that damaged reputation is three and a half years.

If you need any further evidence that what you say and do has a real impact on your business, take a look at these stories, all of which were fuelled by very robust sharing, discussion and commentary across major social media outlets:

- In 2012 nearly $2.2bn was wiped off Goldman Sachs' market value when an employee published a scathing opinion piece in the *New York Times*, openly criticising the CEO and questioning his moral fibre.

- First quarter 2013 sales of Abercrombie & Fitch fell 17% following an ill-advised interview with CEO Mike Jeffries where he suggests the brand is aimed only at "cool kids", sparking outrage among the general public and his own customers.

- In the UK, Tesco's 2013 horsemeat scandal – a major operational issue – wiped £300m off the company's market value.

- In 2012, when a printing firm mistakenly leaked news of a drop in Google's profits early, $24bn was knocked off the value of the company in eight minutes as shares were suspended.

I think "What's the return on reputation-related investment?" is the wrong question to ask. I think you need to be asking instead "What's the risk if we don't invest?" We may not be able to attribute a figure to reputation on our balance sheets – but we know it is there. These – and countless other examples – prove it.

Today's competitive businesses thrive on actionable information – information that can easily be used as a guide to decision-making and organisational planning. Much of this information includes measures or metrics. How many leads did we convert into sales? What is our customer churn rate? What is the average spend per customer?

Reputation is the business's soul

"I don't believe companies think about reputation as much as they should. They use the word 'brand' a lot. Brands are transactional, but reputation is the business's soul."

Brian Cohen, Founder and Chairman, New York Angels and founder Technology Solutions Inc

When it comes to reputation and specifically the discipline of public relations there has been a long-standing issue around measurement: just how do you do it? This isn't surprising, given the intangible nature of the thing. Following on from what Brian Cohen suggests above, measuring reputation is like trying to measure the soul of your business.

On the one hand, you're trying to find out what people think of you now and then measure the result of attempts to improve your reputation. On the other hand, you're trying to measure what impact your reputation has on your results – how do you measure the value that people's perceptions contribute to your business? How do you link your reputation to business metrics like sales and profitability? How much of your marketing effort depends on your reputation?

It is possible to mount an exercise, in my view rather an academic one, to measure the number of column inches or radio and TV time your PR efforts have created and put a value on it – the advertising value equivalents (AVE) as it's known in the industry. However, one thing the PR industry agrees on pretty unanimously is that measuring outputs of media coverage is rather a meaningless exercise. And anyway, reputation goes far, far beyond media coverage of your company. Or even social media conversations and engagement.

Measuring perception is far more useful. Simple perception surveys enable you to benchmark awareness amongst key audiences. This could include, for example, asking a sample of your key prospects questions about their perception of your organisation and its services/products.

You then repeat this exercise at various points during your reputation-building activity (which is ideally always ongoing) and look for trends and progress. Doing this properly and regularly costs quite a lot of money, especially when compared with what a business might spend on PR campaigns overall. I would suggest that you look at all communications activity – outbound marketing, PR, digital campaigns, internal communications – and do a tally of the combined budget. Then set aside 10% of that budget for measurement.

Make sure you are measuring the outcomes that matter to your business, not the metrics that each group wants to measure just because they can. An impressive number is only impressive if it is having a positive impact on your reputation and ultimately your business.

Historically, businesses have concentrated mainly on measuring the impact of public relations. The traditional thinking changes when it comes to measuring the impact of reputation, taking into account social media. Social media has changed the measurement game because every like, click and retweet is so trackable. It's possible to get a view – almost as it happens – of what is being said online about almost anything, if you have the processes in place to do so. That's a lot of input data to monitor and take into account when planning and adjusting your reputation strategy. But beware; social media campaign measurement can be meaningless if it does not link back to business outcomes, real return or profit. The smartest brands are already doing this. Here's one of my favourite examples from the past few years, from Bing Maps.

---

*Case study – appealing to
Twitter followers*

Bing Maps set a marketing goal to increase Microsoft's relevance with the Y generation and to get more people to engage with Bing's new mapping software. The strategy was to appeal to followers of the hip-hop artist Jay-Z. It used the launch of Jay-Z's autobiography as the springboard for activity. As part of the campaign the team 'placed' pages of the yet-to-be-launched book in many locations around the US. Finding these pages meant using Bing Maps to its full potential and so accumulating the book page by page.

The idea generated a phenomenal amount of media attention (online and off), resulting very quickly in Bing becoming one of the world's top-ten most-visited sites. How's that for a meaningful business outcome?

When you start to link the measurement-driven thinking of online campaigns (getting to the top of an online list sells a lot of books), with the more traditional reputation-driven activity (customers recommending you online and off), you start to see the potential to make real changes to your business' fortunes.

STRATEGY WITHOUT
MEASUREMENT IS SHORT-LIVED

As the management consultant Peter Drucker once said, "If you can't measure something, you can't manage it." Nothing is more true when you think about reputation. You're going to spend money on promoting and enhancing your reputation, so in theory you need to know what you're getting back.

So why don't we systematically measure it? The answer is that it's constantly evolving and it's based on things like trust. People buy your products because they trust them and they trust your company. Ideally, we need to find a *before and after* measurement to see whether our customers' trust in us is waxing or waning.

I think the concept of *Net Promoter Score (NPS)* comes closest to measuring what matters. NPS measures the loyalty that exists between a provider and a consumer. The provider can be, for example, a company or an employer. The provider is the entity that is asking the questions on the NPS survey. The consumer is the customer, employee, or respondent to the survey.

NPS is based on a direct question: *How likely are you to recommend our company/product/service to your friends and colleagues?* You can, of course, follow this closed question up with open questions about why the responder has given you the score they have. Despite it having some dissenters, I think that the NPS could be more regularly used as an indicator of the success of reputation-driven campaigns. And perhaps when it comes to reputation, the more interesting metric from NPS is to look at the number of detractors and put all of your focus on them.

If you have done the exercises in Chapter 9, it will have helped to bring to the surface a few key things that are important to your business – and it makes sense that those are the things you measure.

The objectives and plans you included in your strategy will have measureable end points. If the goal you set yourself was to increase sales, make sure you then track the leads generated through both on and offline media and count them. Then look at the rate of increase in sales now compared with the increase in sales before you put the reputation-related activity in place. Perhaps the activity isn't communications-related at all – maybe it is a tweak you have made to widespread behaviour in the customer service department. In this case you will need some sort of feedback mechanism.

Suppose that your goal is to drive down costs. One of the plans to do this might be to track the shift in customer service response from expensive call centres to online self-help. (This is an especially good cost-reducer if you create online forums where customers willingly help each other.) Done well, this strategy should be supported by your reputation-building activity.

If your goal is to enhance your overall reputation, look at the sentiment in what people are saying about you and the share of voice (both online and off) that is given to you compared to your key competitors. In traditional and social media, are people generally positive, negative or neutral in what they say about you? And are the people doing the talking influential?

Cameron Hulett, Managing Director of digital publishing company Undertone, sees reputation as a "datum that should aim to move steadily upwards." He likens social media noise to a regular frequency change across that datum. Sometimes sentiment will be good and sometimes it will be bad – what matters is that you find a way to figure out at what point the negative sentiment is so bad that it will have a long-term, irreparable effect on your reputation, and change your behaviour accordingly. If your behaviour in relation to the negative sentiment is in line with your core values, the chances are that the negative coverage will merely be a storm in a teacup.

You need to work out measures of your own reputation as a whole and of the plans and strategies you have in place to improve it. There simply is no catch-all answer to the measurement question.

> "People's perception of a good reputation has the potential to vary greatly. To choose a topical example in the venture capital world, for one firm an investment in a fast-growing online gambling company is an exciting opportunity. For another, it may be perceived as going against the company's values and result in a tarnished reputation for the investor. It can be a very subjective area, which is what makes the objective measure of reputation so difficult."
>
> **Davor Hebel, Partner, Fidelity Growth Partners Europe**

LISTEN, LISTEN, LISTEN TO SOCIAL MEDIA

Social media is an absolute goldmine of information for any business. It gives you direct, real-time insight into the opinions being expressed about your company, your products, or issues that matter to you. But, and it's a big but, you only get the benefit if you listen to those insights in the right way. You need to think logically and laterally about what might be useful to you.

For example, suppose your business makes turbines for wind farms and you are bidding for an upcoming wind farm project against stiff competition. By its very nature the project is likely to encounter some local and even national resistance.

A careful audit of online conversations about the project gives you solid insights into general public opinion. This might influence any recommendations you include in the proposal about how you will communicate to these communities throughout the build process, should you win. Use your reputation; include a case study of another project you worked on where there were similar issues that were handled well. Engage with concerned communities (online and off) in a human way. Use social media not only as a platform for content distribution, but to have meaningful conversations.

You've got to listen in order to understand and influence the bigger picture. There are ways to track the most influential voices on any given topic, on social media, and potentially reach out to them directly. Twitter includes a number of case studies on its development website to help businesses see how they might effectively use the platform to drive their own business (**dev.twitter.com/case-studies**). This one, about finding and appealing to the right audiences in a measurable way, caught my attention:

Finding the right people, saying the right thing

Feeding America is the leading domestic hunger relief charity in the United States, helping more than 37 million low-income individuals each year. The charity uses Twitter to drive awareness about hunger alleviation efforts, share key news and statistics, highlight celebrity partnerships and rally citizens to action.

Feeding America wanted to maximise traffic from Twitter to its website by aligning its tweets with popular topics and their existing content.

Its solution was to partner with Performics, the Global Performance Marketing Agency, and search optimisation specialist BrightEdge to review the volume of tweets, search engine rankings and web analytics. Based on the data they collected, they determined what they should tweet about and what type of content their tweets should link to on their website. As a result, Feeding America yielded more than double the average traffic levels per post on the optimised tweets, relative to standard tweets made in the same period.

Whether you believe your business has reason to engage in social media or not, I believe very strongly that every single company should be listening actively to what is being said. In doing so you will gain:

- An understanding of the sentiment felt about a product/service.

- An understanding of any issue directly or indirectly linked to your success.

- Competitive insight.

- Employee insight.

- A way to tap into new talent (and the list goes on...).

There are hundreds of companies out there that offer 24-hour monitoring and will create reports that are specifically tailored to your needs. Many offer real-time social media monitoring and analysis. These reports will be worth every pound/dollar/yen you spend. Used properly they will help you to understand and quickly respond to significant conversations about your company or its brands. As I said in Chapter 13, don't wait for a crisis to find a monitoring partner.

So why are so many businesses still failing to listen to what social media is telling them?

Fear is the first reason and this is not always without justification – there can be some nasty stuff said out there. But the way a company chooses to respond to comments says just as much about the company as its quarterly results used to; it's the company's shop window, whether you like it or not.

The other major fear is that if a company enters the realm of social media and encourages employee activity, it will somehow *spark* a crisis. In reality, any crisis that does arise is much more likely to emanate from a fundamental misalignment of your company's values and behaviour. Yes, social media may be the channel through which unfortunate information spreads. If that happens, you **need** to know so that you can deal with it.

The smartest companies see negative commentary on social media as a positive opportunity to turn dissenters into ambassadors, based on the response that they get from the company. The quality of this response happens as a result of culture and if you don't listen to what's being said, you may not even be aware that a culture shift is necessary.

SETTING A BENCHMARK
FOR SUCCESS

Perhaps the most difficult benchmark to create in the reputation economy involves the core values of the company. How do you measure how well your company, at every level and in every department, consistently demonstrates its core beliefs?

The reputation steering committee should have some measures in place for this in reputation management strategy, but senior managers can use their own antennae to get a feel, if not a statistic, for what's going on. Shop floor visits, mystery shoppers and experiencing the job application process are all activities that keep leadership close to the reality of the company's interaction with its stakeholders. Find out what it feels like to do business with you.

Let's look at the banks as one example: with the difficult economic conditions experienced between 2007 and 2013 (and expected to continue for some months and possibly years), it was particularly important for company boards to keep their finger on the pulse of the realities of economic life. At a time of price inflation on the one hand and zero or below zero wage inflation on the other, the gap between people doing well and people being badly squeezed was widening.

As a result, there was a lot of publicity about the high-profile bonuses that some companies pay their senior people. Senior managers would have been well advised to not only hear the resultant grumbling but to check that they were avoiding any such animosity in their own business and any possibility of that sort of publicity. But remember, in anything like this behaviour is the real key: if the reality is that pay is disproportionate, changing how you communicate about it is unlikely to have much effect.

Use the data available to monitor the issues that are key to your business and track the general perception shift. If you don't see a positive trend, maybe it's time to take a harder look at what you are doing internally that is reflecting poorly to the outside world. My advice is not to start with the communications team: start with the business function that is at the root of the issue.

REPUTATION/PERCEPTION
AUDIT

Now let's move to a more concrete level of benchmark. If a business is going to do any measurement at all, I believe the priority should be a reputation/perception audit, conducted regularly, among the specific audiences that matter to your company. The insight is very powerful. Such an audit has seven steps:

1. Gaining internal agreement on who your key stakeholders are.

2. Getting bullet point lists of the attributes that your research should include from internal and external stakeholders.

3. Designing the research questionnaire for your stakeholders, ensuring that it will meet everyone's requirements.

4. Analysing the findings and producing clear reports.

5. Submitting the research results to the reputation steering committee.

6. Disseminating the information necessary from the research for the relevant teams to create action plans.

7. Agreeing the actions necessary to improve the reputation and perception of your company.

The research findings will contribute to the reputation benchmark and create a platform for regular, consistent research to measure a change in either direction.

So, what does successful measurement look like? Remember that fundamentally we're still trying to measure reputation. This has many different guises; one size does not fit all. For instance, Ryanair and Microsoft wouldn't be looking to measure the same attributes, and that's not just because of the difference in industry. Both companies have very different core values. If you don't care about customer service, measuring what people think about your company's customer service is money down the drain.

Reputation measurement boils down to measuring values versus customer experience – and the gap that may exist between the two. Every report that includes data gained by listening to social and other media should end with a recommendation for what the people affected should do.

MEASUREMENT TOOLS

There are countless measurement tools on the market and new ones are introduced regularly. But to give you a flavour of what's possible, I've identified three that demonstrate the varied approaches you might take to external measurement of the things that matter most to your company.

The Reputation Quotient

One very interesting initiative over the past few years is the creation of a Reputation Quotient by Harris Interactive (HI). Its starting point was a definition of corporate reputation:

"Corporate Reputation can be defined as the sum of all perceptions and expectations that relevant stakeholders have about a company in relation to that specific stakeholder's own agenda."

It has tried to find the one-size fits all benchmark by stating the key pillars of reputation: products and services, emotional appeal, vision and leadership, financial performance, workplace environment and social responsibility. As a foundation these are excellent and they provide the perfect starting point for discussion among the reputation planning team.

Harris has gone a long way to creating a benchmark that works across industry and it is a huge leap in the right direction compared with things like the currently used advertising value equivalent (AVE) measure.

There is more detail about the Reputation Quotient on the Harris Interactive website (**www.harrisinteractive.com/Ins ights/2013RQStudyExecutiveSummary.aspx**).

Edelman's trust barometer

The other initiative that I believe captures the essence of reputation management is Edelman's *trust barometer*. In its latest survey – of 30,000 people in 26 countries – Edelman gauges the general population's trust in institutions (including government and enterprise), industries and leaders. The findings are fascinating and I'd encourage any business leader to read them. You can find the 2013 results on the Edelman website (**www. edelman.com/trust-downloads/global-results-2**).

The RepTrack Pulse

Finally, it is worth taking a look at the Reputation Institute's RepTrak Pulse tool (**www.reputationinstitute.com/thought-leadership**). It is a system that measures the levels of trust, admiration, good feeling and overall esteem that important stakeholders feel towards your business. Although I've not had direct experience with the tool myself, it appears to have the academic rigour behind it to make the output meaningful.

IDENTIFY AND MEASURE
THE THINGS THAT
MATTER MOST

Ultimately, in order for your reputation strategy to be successful, you need to identify the things that matter most and measure them in a way that makes sense for you. The basic benchmark I've suggested you can create internally (outlined in Chapter 9) does away with siloed reporting from all the different functions – marketing, PR, customer service and so on – and creates a consolidated benchmark that includes every aspect of your reputation. If you want something more sophisticated it is well worth exploring options like NPS and the varied reports outlined above.

Despite lots of potentially conflicting advice and differing opinions when it comes to reputation management, everyone agrees that measurement of the impact of reputation must be measured by outcomes – genuine contribution to business goals. So make that the starting point for any discussion.

ASK YOUR TEAM...

- Do we already do a perception audit among stakeholders? If so, what does it tell us? And do we act on it?

- Do we have social media monitoring in place? And if so, does it contain actionable recommendations based on findings?

- Are we clear on what areas of our business need most attention?

CHAPTER 17

Reputation
and the
Bottom Line

THE STARTING POINT FOR
MEASURING
OVERALL REPUTATION

Measuring progress in maintaining and improving your reputation starts from where you are now. It must be woven into the plan, as I highlighted at the beginning of the *Playbook*. But we don't operate in a vacuum. As you consider your own reputation journey, where you are now, and where you want to be, make sure you take the right context into account. Not only the general perception of your industry (the reputation of companies in the financial services industry will have a different starting point than companies in the technology sector), but the perception of the market as a whole.

Consider all the stakeholders – anyone who is in any way involved in what your organisation is up to has an impact on your reputation. And then there's what's fashionable – today sustainability, tomorrow tax propriety and so on. These things will differ depending on your industry and accepted norms within it. By its very nature, it is a moving goal post. You need to identify what is most important to you and look at it consistently, over time. Don't expect change to happen overnight.

The key is in creating an effective feedback system bringing up-to-date information concerning everything that's significant in maintaining and advancing your reputation. From *every* area of the business.

If you don't have sophisticated systems in place to do this and haven't engaged with one of the reputation management experts I mentioned in the previous chapter, my recommendation is to use the questions I have posed throughout to define your starting point. You'll know quite quickly what matters to your business and what's less relevant.

I have derived a starter list from the questions I've been posing at the end of each chapter as a basis for thought. But even better than this, go back to the questions that struck a chord with you most and compile them into your own list.

QUESTIONS TO ASK TO HELP DEFINE YOUR STARTING POINT

Product/ service quality	Have you defined your why (purpose) and your core values? Is company and employee behaviour always aligned with that purpose and your values? How do you know?
Customer service	Are you using social media as a critical customer service channel and if so are you tracking the data?
Environmental/ sustainability issues	Is your behaviour in this area consistent with your values? Are you vulnerable to any adverse comment? Are there skeletons in your closet?
Financial performance	Is your finance-related behaviour (salaries/bonuses/tax) in line with your values? Are you monitoring specific incidences of reputation-related activity having an impact on financial performance (good or bad)? Do you track important investors' online conversations?
Business governance	Have you run a reputation planning meeting driven by the company goals and core values? Is social media part of your governance and compliance? If not, should it be? Have you re-evaluated your crisis plans and examined the potential role social media might play?
Independent review	Have you done a reputation/perception audit?
Employee satisfaction and engagement	Is your senior team well-versed in the impact of social media on reputation? Is everyone aware of the simply stated and illustrated culture of your organisation? Is it being reflected in behaviour – from the receptionist to the CFO and everywhere in between? How do you reward self-driven brand ambassadors?
Communications strategy	Is the company's desired reputation clearly stated and understood internally? Does your communications team have examples to support your desired reputation? Are you following a reputation management process? Are the key messages you are sending out thought-through and supported by proof statements? Is there a plan for external communication and does everyone who should know about it?

Answering (and rating out of ten) the questions against each attribute takes your measurement to a logical basis of where you are now, from the gut feel of Chapter 2. It might be interesting to reflect this in the **Radar chart of reputation issues** on page 113, and see how it compares to the first one you did.

Based on this benchmark, you at least have a starting point for putting into place both hard and soft measures for the reputation steering committee to report on to the board. And as the CEO, you have an at-a-glance view of where the trouble spots are.

JUSTIFYING RESOURCES FOR REPUTATION ACTIVITIES

While almost everyone accepts that there is a strong direct relationship between reputation and share price, it feels pretty near impossible to estimate the financial benefits of spending money specifically on an organisation's reputation. And yet, it has to be done.

In calculating the return on investment in reputation-related activity there may well be dramatic inaccuracies. In fact, some of the certainties in the plan will quite possibly come to nothing; but the individual you have made accountable for your reputation, supported by the steering committee, still needs to go through the process of estimating the additional revenue and costs of any new expenditure in the reputation arena. The benefits of applying this discipline are:

- It gives a rough idea of the financial consequences of implementing a reputation strategy.

- It makes certain that the people involved have thought through reputation issues thoroughly.

- Managers can make their best estimates and then weigh them for risk.

- It gives the basis for a *contract*, albeit a loose one, between the board and the director concerned with reputation.

- It allows people from different disciplines on the board to give feedback to the Chief Reputation Officer, both their gut feel on the strategy and lessons they have learnt about valuing reputation in the past.

- It ensures that the flair and inventiveness of the people coming up with new ideas has been exposed to the realities of business and that they can stand up to questions posed by you, the CEO.

REPUTATION SPEND – WHERE DOES IT COME FROM?

The answer for where reputation spend comes from is simple: everywhere. Arguably all marketing and PR activity is supporting reputation. But what about structural changes made to the way customer service is handled? If it is being done to better support the business's values and purpose, make that clear. If you do, eventually managers see the resources they put into reputation filtering back into their bottom line.

In most businesses, people in leadership require a business case whenever someone asks for financial resources for any sort of speculative activity – targeting a new market for example. Some successful managers are not fazed by a request for a business case no matter how difficult it may appear to write at first. How, for example, do you measure return on investment in manning the Twitter feed 24/7? Well, with some difficulty, but logically if a manager cannot connect expenditure on resourcing a 24/7 operation to their business objectives, why are they putting the cover there in the first place? And perhaps the case to put forward is not the revenue generation, but the opportunity cost of not doing so – think back to the British Airways example.

I don't mean to suggest that measuring the impact of reputation on the bottom line is easy. Calculating the return on investment on reputation-focused activities is a difficult combination of art and science, but I do maintain that everyone should aim to do it, and that everyone should aim to work in a logical fashion, with the occasional leap of faith and imagination.

As a starting point, ask your key people this:

- Given your understanding of our reputation and our values, what resources financial and otherwise have you put into its protection and exploitation?

- What has been the financial result?

Such an exercise puts a manager into the required frame of mind. It asks your business managers to separate reputation expenditure from the rest of their budget and show how it has gone through to the bottom line. And if the bottom line is one step too far, look at other, very specific measures, like Dell's focus on converting 'ranters' to 'ravers'. This is unquestionably tied to the business's reputation.

SOCIAL MEDIA SPEND – JUSTIFY IT

Measuring the return on social media/digital spend is infinitely easier – because the data is so readily available if you look for it. Ensure you have the right tracking systems in place, not only to track things like click-throughs, but ultimately the most interesting measure is conversion rates. Do you have the systems in place to do this?

Outputs and outtakes are not in and of themselves valuable. Output is from the company: content, news releases, coverage and so on. Outtake is the extent to which the audience has engaged, measured by follows, retweets, shares, media coverage.

Outputs and outtakes reveal only superficial insight. They don't show how you have *shifted the needle* when it comes to business or reputation progress, and don't show value to the business. Outcomes measured against outputs and outtakes are a better measure of the success (or otherwise) of social media activity and ROI. Or any communications activity for that matter. That's why deciding your desired outcomes at the start of the process is so important.

ASK YOURSELF/YOUR TEAM...

- Are we really measuring what matters? Or are we being distracted by the things that are *easiest* to measure?

- Are we tracking progress against an initial benchmark?

- Are we measuring our reputation among all priority stakeholders, including employees?

Conclusion

Whether you've worked through the book from start to finish, or dipped in and out of the chapters that resonated most with you and your current business challenge, I hope you've learned something along the way.

With the dawn of social media, it is safe to say that reputation management will never be the same again. The power to make or break your company's reputation lies firmly in the hands of all those you interact with. But shaping their perceptions is up to you. Whether you choose to embrace social media or not, it will have an impact on how you and your business are perceived. Can you afford to ignore it?

As CEO of a business, the important thing is not that you know the ins and outs of social media, but simply that you 'get it' and its importance when it comes to your reputation. And critically, acknowledging the significance of acting in line with your core values, across every area of your business, ensures that you are minimising the risk of damage to your reputation. A company that is seen to 'do the right thing' time and again will build up enormous goodwill among important stakeholders, and for good reason.

When it comes to corporate reputation management, no one has all the answers. But I do believe that those business leaders who ask the right questions are the ones who will win in the long run.

I have created free templates relating to things I've addressed in the *Playbook* for you to download at **www.thereputationplaybook.com**. And if you have stories you'd like to share about your own experiences, I'd love to hear them.

Good luck!

INDEX